A NOT-SO-TENDER OFFER

AN INSIDER'S LOOK AT MERGERS AND THEIR CONSEQUENCES

ISADORE BARMASH

PRENTICE HALL
Englewood Cliffs, New Jersey 07632

Prentice-Hall International (UK) Limited, *London*
Prentice-Hall of Australia Pty. Limited, *Sydney*
Prentice-Hall Canada, Inc., *Toronto*
Prentice-Hall Hispanoamericana, S.A., *Mexico*
Prentice-Hall of India Private Limited, *New Delhi*
Prentice-Hall of Japan, Inc., *Tokyo*
Simon & Schuster Asia Pte. Ltd., *Singapore*
Editora Prentice-Hall do Brasil, Ltda., *Rio de Janeiro*

© 1995 by
PRENTICE-HALL
Englewood Cliffs, NJ

10 9 8 7 6 5 4 3 2 1

Library of Congress Cataloging-in-Publication Data

Barmash, Isadore
   A not so tender offer : an insider's look at mergers and their conse-
quences / by Isadore Barmash.
       p. cm.
   ISBN 0-13-182312-4 (cloth).
   1. Consolidation and merger of corporations—United States. 2. Tender
offers (Securities)—United States. 3. Leveraged buyouts—United States.
   4. Corporations—United States—Finance. I. Title.
HD2746.55.U537   1995
338.8'3—dc20   95-18574
                                                                CIP

ISBN 0-13-182312-4

PRENTICE HALL
Career & Personal Development
Englewood Cliffs, NJ 07632

A Simon & Schuster Company

Printed in the United States of America

For Sarah, Elaine, Stanley, Marilyn, and Pamela

Contents

Part One—Merger Mania

Chapter 1
Why Are These Mergers Different from All Other Mergers?
(3)

Chapter 2
When the Urge to Merge Becomes the Zest to Divest (19)

Chapter 3
The Strategic Merger (33)

Part Three—The People Who Make It Happen

Part Four—*Financing the Merger*

Preface

Tender—The offer of money or performance in connection with a contract, if unjustifiably refused, places the party who refused in default and gives rise to an action for breach of contract. (Financial Services Handbook, Jones Lang Wooton)

Every day and often several times a day, American corporations are merging with or acquiring companies in a breeding frenzy that seems to have no end. Sometimes, their reasons are obvious and sometimes they strain logic. But always, they contain a dimension of drama, business people trying desperately to expand their business in aggressive moves that in turn affect many other people, their families, livelihoods and the economies of their cities and towns.

The mosaic of implicit and explicit factors involved in mergers is rich and varied indeed: size, industry, internal conditions, external conditions, government scrutiny, stock market values, the effect on stockholders, the effect on employees, the effect on the local economies, the ability to digest the transaction, the ultimate cost of the transaction and many other considerations. All these form equations that differ in each case, not unlike the protagonists themselves regardless of whether it is a friendly or unfriendly deal.

In the buying binge, no major industry is omitted. Defense. Telecommunications. Banking. Media Book publishing. Pharmaceuticals. Health care. Railroads. Retailing. Entertainment. Computers. Packaged goods. The goals are expansion, boosting market share, achieving the benefits of economy of scale, reducing costs, preparing for global expansion. In this fourth wave of corporate mergers since 1920, one of the surprising differences this time around is that few people seem concerned that all the mergers and acquisitions—M&As—might be creating excesses, anticompetitive forces and people abuses. Government opposition is minimal. Academics are no longer militant. Activists are quiescent. Unions only occasionally clear their throats. So silence reigns amid the rumble of the merger machine.

In fact, as television viewers and newspaper readers blithely take in the latest "tender offer," it's hard not to accept that it is all woven now into our national fabric—buying is cheaper and faster than building. It brings instant growth, and hopefully certain, eventual success. This concept has become so intrinsically American, so logical, sensible and "decent" from a business and common-sense standpoint that it is now a vital weapon in the American business armament. Much has happened in the merger arena since my earlier book on mergers, "Welcome to Our Conglomerate—You're Fired!" (1971). The conglomerates which created new corporate formations in the 1960s and 1970s were succeeded by leveraged buyouts in the 1980s and deconglomerization in the 1980s and 1990s. Now, it's the strategic merger, quite possibly the most promising concept in M&As that has appeared in decades.

Maybe it's because there just have been too many mergers and too many with blue-chip names or because everyone is convinced that the American economy badly needs a shaking out, a recycling, that most people see it as a way to compete more effectively in the new global economy. No one would argue with that. But there's considerable legitimacy in the names that dominate the recent M&A trend—AT&T, Bell Atlantic, Lockheed, Martin Marietta, Tele-Communications, McCaw Electronics, Time Warner, General Electric, CBS, NBC, Eli Lilly, Merck & Company, for just a few. And legitimacy, let's face it squarely, leads to acceptance.

In terms of pure numbers, the peak year in M&As was 1989 when the value of such business consolidations totalled $457 billion, a lot of it due to the popularity of junk bonds. The value of transactions fell sharply in the years from 1990 through 1992 but partly bounced back to $359 billion in 1993. In the first eight months of 1994, M&As had a value of about $210 billion. But the main difference is the immensely larger size of such recent-year deals as the RJR Nabisco merger for $30 billion and the Bell Atlantic Tele-Communications deal for $33 billion which happened to abort. But size was—and is—no problem to merger makers.

The aim of this book is two-fold. One objective is to show how the "species mergers Americanus circa 1990s" evolved from the conglomerate binge into one that has assumed equal

rank with internal expansion in much of American business—
the merger or acquisition which adds related businesses to each
other to create a better, but somehow leaner whole. Among the
subjects covered: Why the current batch is different from past
versions. Why conglomerates mostly didn't work and how they
are scurrying to divest what they once dearly craved. What really is a strategic merger? Is there intrinsically a philosophy of
mergers? How an actual, typical merger evolved and was successfully concluded in a surprising way. Why are there so many
foreign deals? And, are hostile transactions really coming back?

The book's second objective is to raise some questions
about the effect of M&A's on people and whether rampant size
might not be a matter of concern. Hence, there are chapters on
the "circus-like" atmosphere of some mergers, as well as predictions of job losses and forecasts about the outlook by eight of
the nation's most thoughtful professionals close to the merger
scene. The point of this second objective: is bigger good and
even bigger better?

There are many stories and people here: a hundred or more
actual stories, case histories, ancedotes; Wall Street's new, newer
and newest breeds; the big M&A players and the "little players"
who ply the more modest cities of America putting together the
small businesses that are the real marrow of American business.

As you read this book, I hope you will enjoy a nutritious
combination: a lot of information, an anecdotal feast, food for
thought and—a little suspense.

Prologue: The Ultimate Acquisition

As he waited tensely by the high-priority telephone in the Oval Office, the young man who had carried 240 million Americans on his back for the last year with a smiling, toothy ease was extremely annoyed with himself.

He should have known or sensed, he told himself, what was about to happen. Not that he really knew what it was, only that undoubtedly it would be unpleasant, threatening, possibly dangerous. "Shoot," he kept repeating, "shoot." Rueful but sympathetic smiles appeared on the faces of the three men who sat facing him. They knew when he was really upset and he was.

The warnings, they responded, were clearly connected now in retrospect but had not been individually linked before.

The first—was it really only two weeks ago?—had been a most unusual blip in the purchase of Treasury notes and bonds by a new investment company with offices in the American Virgin Islands. Several hundred millions of dollars worth in the original purchase had mushroomed in a few days to more than $10 billion worth. Government and media curiosity had proved fruitless. In the end, they had decided that the Caribbean financial company was merely a cover for some Mideast sheiks and bankers to shore up a fund in the event the fading dollar would finally show some ambition and strengthen.

The next sign, all so clear in retrospect, was a similar, large-scale purchase of common stock in the bluest of blue chips—IBM, AT&T, General Electric, General Motors, Wal-Mart Stores, Procter & Gamble. But since the original buy was placed on one of the year's heaviest trading days on Wall Street, the purchase by a new Swiss pension fund aroused little attention. Nor had it when the same buyers continued to remain active for days afterward.

The third sign was a rare, one-day scooping up of considerable available real estate through private transactions and from the Resolution Trust Corporation auctioning of distress properties enmeshed in the tangle of savings-and-loan companies. Since many of these transactions were by different, obscure companies, they, too, like the others, slid under the door without arousing more than a glimmer of scrutiny. After all, didn't everyone want the real estate business to revive?

xiii

The fourth, and what should have been the real tipoff that something very odd and sinister was brewing, was a series of advisories from principal U.S. allies that some of their primary banks and insurance companies were being surveyed by a new Luxembourg consulting group about whether they would consider funding major purchases of certain American assets. These included the Chrysler and Woolworth buildings in New York, the Sears Tower in Chicago, the John Hancock Center in Boston and such shopping centers as the Mall of America in Bloomington, Minnesota, the King-of-Prussia Shopping Center in Pennsylvania and the Ala Moana Mall in downtown Honolulu. But since this had involved only inquiries but not purchases, it had generated little concern at the White House so that the matter was directed to the Secretary of Commerce. But he was otherwise engaged in Tokyo where he was again vainly twisting arms to open Japan to more reciprocal trade.

That had been the penultimate signal.

However, neither the President nor the core of his staff failed to miss the ultimate signal that followed the initial four.

The message was direct, if cryptic. Received on a low-priority computer line into the White House communications network, the message had produced increasing consternation as it had proceeded up through the White House communications hierarchy. It was addressed to "The President" and consisted of a baffling but concise nine words.

"Treasuries. Equities. Properties. Advisories.

Expect call Friday, 5:30 p.m. EST."

They waited expectantly, but no call came.

Finally, on Sunday, the overdue message of explanation arrived not by telephone but by fax. Its quiet appearance, however, belied its import. In the Oak Office, the President and the three men read it together, hardly believing what it said. The sheer audacity of it caught in their throats so that for a few moments each found it difficult to breathe. After they had all read it once, the President read it again out loud:

Mr. President—

"This will serve notice that an international consortium formed for the purpose of acquisition wishes to make a friendly offer to acquire the United States of America. By anonymous transactions in the last two weeks, we have already acquired a very substantial stake in the American infrastructure and intend to add to it. Other than the United States government and its citizens, we are the largest owner of American properties although the share at present is still quite small. Make no mistake and do not scoff at our intentions. We are very, very serious. What we propose is a meeting to take place at any mutually agreeable site to discuss our plan with you and your administration in a productive manner so that the American citizens receive full value for their constitutional rights. We suggest that you make a public announcement of this and also of your decision. Once we see what that is, you will hear further from us."

It was unsigned.

Everything at the White House went into high gear. The top-level meeting was transferred from the Oval Office to a conference room with a long table where the President sat at its head, puffing thoughtfully on his cigar and finally more at ease than he had been since the earlier message had arrived hours and hours ago. "A wild, crazy-all threat to take over the whole ball game," he told the 20-some faces. "Who would have thought it? An' what the blank kind of 'international consortium'? Where do they get the guts to do it? There's no precedent for it in history!"

The Commerce Secretary and the Treasury Secretary both spoke at once.

"Mr. President, business consolidations are running rampant everywhere and it's a virus that can strike anywhere," pontificated the Commerce Secretary. "Who can place parameters of size and degree on it? There's no such thing as just a mega-merger anymore—but mega, mega, mega!"

"Mr. President, this event is a function of our weak dollar," the Treasury Secretary began. "Wild they may be but these people have captured the very best timing to make a stab at us. Our dollar is the weakest it's been in two years. Sir, we are simply a great bargain!"

"Bargain my foot!" snapped the Secretary of State, who was uncharacteristically undiplomatic. "Let's tell these countries or radicals to take a flying leap! What are they talking about? You can't acquire a country, can you?"

"You can by military force," said the Secretary of Defense.

"The other big countries look at us as a fading giant," said the Treasury Secretary, the Cabinet's pragmatist, "and the little countries are snapping at our heels. This idea of buying the U.S.—absolutely ridiculous at the very least—is a natural development considering our loss of international stature. I say—"

A metallic voice pierced through his meditation. It was the President's communications director, a former Texas newsman who had been with him since the President had been a lowly state legislator. "Mr. President, if we keep a lid on all this," the P.R. man said in his rasping voice (the President in 20 years had never really gotten used to it) "how will this international consortium know what our reaction is?"

The common-sense question abruptly cleared the President's mind and caused everyone slumping around the table to straighten up. No one had any suggestions. Finally, the President said, "Maybe the best approach is to ignore them. That should either smoke them out or make them go away. Right?" Everyone slowly nodded.

During the next few days, the President took action aimed at shoring up the "American defense." And he put some considerable heat under other investigative efforts to determine who or what group had generated the message and various purchases. But, again, nothing. When the following Sunday arrived without any developments, he told his closest associates, "Whoever it is either is playing a game of nerves or has gone back into his booby hatch to play basketball with his head. Personally, I favor the second."

But he was wrong. That night, top executives of the New York Times, the Washington Post and the Wall Street Journal call him to inform him of a full-page "tombstone" advertisement appearing in the next morning's pages. Amazingly, they told him—and later read him—the announcement to "The Great American Public" that each American family would be offered $1 million to sign a release of its ownership rights in The nation's assets. In addition, the still unidentified consortium was making a direct offer to the United States government of $50 trillion in "the hardest of currencies and most reliable notes" to surrender its ownership and holdings. The ads assured the public that any transaction of the kind would be entirely legal. More details would be forthcoming in a week, the ads said, during which time Americans could discuss the matter with their families, their legislators, attorneys and spiritual advisors. The ads also noted that the $1 million payment per American family, most of whom had never earned more than $20,000 a year, was lavish indeed and could even be made tax-free if the government would cooperate.

Bitterly swallowing his disappointment that the initiative had been stolen from him, the President went on national television and radio at 10 that night.

"My fellow Americans," he said, finding his vision misty but trying to keep the raw emotion out of his voice, "you and I have received an unusual offer to sell what we own as a natural birthright. It is what is known as a 'tender' offer. But in this case, my friends, it is a 'not so tender' offer because if enough of you accept it, you will lose everything..."

part one

_____

Merger Mania

chapter 1

Why are These Mergers Different from All Other Mergers?

A hostile offer to acquire the United States (as described in the Prologue) is a fantastic idea, admittedly. Could it actually happen?

If the new global economy of the mid- and late 1990s is a practical concept—and it is—just how remote is an economic takeover of an entire country? Putting it another way, if powerful nations like Japan, China and Germany have vowed to give up military exploitation, would they not be likely to replace it with economic exploitation? I do not mean that these three individually or in combination would mount a takeover of another country. I mean only that economic takeovers are possible on a grand scale, given the new weapons of dynamic economic expansion and wide open financing capability to support it the world round, not to mention some exploding human urges like the yearning for more room in which to live, breathe and grow. What might all that lead to?

As any frequent traveler to Europe knows, the German language and German products confront one on every side, particularly in Switzerland, Hungary and the Czech Republic. Defeated in two major wars. Germany is now the economic, if not the cultural colossus of Europe. We need not dwell on the great international clout that Japan has achieved despite its defeat in the 1940s, advancing economically to stake claims in Asia, North America and Europe. Singly or together, they represent a very formidable rival to the United States, as will China in just a few more years.

But there's another factor that supersedes the unlikely with the probable.

The buy-not-build theory has sunk deep roots. Not very long ago in this country and in most other developed countries, it was normal to open a business, a plant, a farm, a store. In fact, the start-up trend was for many years the basic way to grow. But in the last few decades, buying someone else's work has replaced the start-up. Why not? It's cheaper in the long run, faster, more likely to yield a good return, and gives one instant entry wherever the business is. And it is catching on in Europe and surely will elsewhere as foreign businessmen watch the American antics.

Needless to say, the merger-and-acquisition trend has erupted in every industry—from banks to funeral homes, from stores to advertising agencies, from television networks to airlines. The shuffling within and without industries has been almost dazzling as every day's financial pages seems to unveil yet another deal.

Recently, as I accompanied my wife to the area's shopping malls, I would find myself playing a game that only served to irritate her. As we passed each chain's branch store, whether it was Kinney, Foot Locker, Sports Authority, Office Max, Fashion Bug, J.A. Riggings or Banana Republic, I would inform her with all the authority of my long business-writing background, "See that Kinney, that's really Woolworth. Sports Authority, that's K Mart. Riggings, that Edison Bros. out of St. Louis. Fashion Bug, that's Charming ..." Inevitably, my wife, one of America's great consumers, would pull me short. "Will that help me get a better price or better service?" she would demand.

Before I could reply in one particular instance, my eye fell on another store, and I was suddenly confused as to which company owned it. The retail chain of which that was a branch had changed hands three times in five years. And just as suddenly, I wasn't sure about some of the others, either. "You know," I told my wife, "if all this backing and shuffling continues, soon I won't be able to tell you who belongs to what anymore." It hardly takes any guesswork to know what she said to that.

Transactions Are Up but Dollar Values Are Down

In researching this book, one of the most intriguing things I found was the vast difference in opinion about whether we are indeed in a major merger trend or whether we are merely seeing the momentum of a peak reached back in 1989. The prime reason for debate is the fact that while the numbers of merger transactions in the United States are up substantially, the total dollar value of mergers is down from the record year but nonetheless rising.

In 1989, for example, the value of all M&As totaled $457 billion, many of the deals reflecting the explosion in the use of junk or high-interest bonds used for financing them. Two and three years later, in 1991 and 1992, the value in each year plummeted to about $290 billion, reflecting in reverse the decline in the use of the junk bonds. But in 1993, it rose 24 percent to $359 billion as new financing vehicles were generated.

But between 1989 and 1993, the number of transactions rose from 10,800 to 14,600. And despite some of the megamergers of the last two years, the percentage of transactions valued at over $1 billion fell in the 1989-1993 time span. In 1989, deals worth at least $1 billion represented 46 percent of the total transactions. By 1992, the percentage fell to 23 percent. But in 1993, it rose again to about 38 percent of the total.

As Steven Rattner, senior vice president of Lazard Freres, the well-known New York investment bankers, put it: "The smaller percentage of $1 billion-plus deals does show the impact of the reduction in large transactions. But, nonetheless, the fact that there were 4,000 more deals in 1993 than in 1989 shows that mergers are very popular in American business."

So, is there a big merger trend under way as the 1990s reach their midpoint? Yes, in numbers, not so in big deals—yet. But what about the big, multi-billion-dollar deals like RJR Nabisco, AT&T and McCaw Electronics, Paramount Communications and Viacom and CBS and QVC?

Well, we come to the major differences between the most recent mergers and those of a few years earlier. The differences are vast.

To begin with, the mergers and acquisitions of the 1990s differ from the mostly financially-driven variety of the 1980s and 1970s in being much more strategically oriented. Now an AT&T buys a McCaw Electronics because it wants to add a major cellular phone maker to its existing manufacturing and service ability in telephones. Viacom, the big cable and TV shopping operator, buys Paramount Communications (Paramount Productions, Simon and Schuster, etc.) because it wants to share in the entertainment and communications businesses. Federated Department Stores, seeking to expand its market share, makes a successful bid to acquire R.H. Macy. These are all strategic deals aimed at expanding in identical or related fields.

So, the new version is entrepreneurial in nature as opposed to the old version which represented pure investment through either diversification or shotgun additions. A specific example: Before its 1986 merger with Nabisco Inc., RJR Industries, the big tobacco products company, had bought Sea-Land (the freight forwarder) Heublein (Smirnov vodka, Inglenook wines, Kentucky Fried Chicken) as well as a motley collection of other non-tobacco-related companies. But when Ross Johnson came from Nabisco to head the merged company, he sold off many of the non-related entities. Thus, RJR, which had bought its way into "conglomeritis" to escape the sting of the tobacco-cancer threat, shifted in the late 1980s and 1990s into a much more cohesive, entrepreneurial company. The fact that most experts consider the RJR-Nabisco merger an unsuccessful one probably indicates that the company's divestiture isn't over; getting rid of the basic tobacco business may be the next, irrevocable step.

But the RJR-Nabisco example proved no dampener on merger-and-acquisition players. After a hectic 1994 merger year, 1995's trend showed plenty of vigor.

In a move that stunned many with its surprise and scope, Kirk Kerkorian, the soft-spoken but aggressive investor-buyer of airlines, movie companies and Las Vegas casinos, announced in mid-April a $22 billion offer for Chrysler Corporation. Already the largest Chrysler shareholder with 10 percent of its stock, Kerkorian said that he and Lee Iacocca, the former Chrysler chairman, would head the buying group. But a shocked Chrysler board quickly convened and responded that the company was not for sale. The deal, which shaped up as a form of leveraged buyout, would have been one of the largest mergers in history.

Only a week before a done deal stirred both the Hollywood and chemical industries. Seagram Company, the big Canadian and United States distiller, agreed to sell most of its stake in the DuPont Corporation for $8.8 billion and moved to acquire 80 percent of MCA, Inc., the movie and entertainment conglomerate, for about $7 billion. The twin transactions indicated a shift on the part of Edgar Bronfman, Jr., and his family who controlled Seagram away from beverages, distilled spirits and chemicals to the movie and music businesses. Wide ripples were expected from this transfer of MCA's ownership from Matsushita in Japan to Seagram's and its perky 39-year-old chairman.

Other striking buyouts in the new year included a $2 billion takeover of Kemper Corporation by a Zurich investment group; Donald Trump and his lenders' sale of control of New York City's plush Plaza Hotel to Prince Walid bin Talal of Saudi Arabia and Singapore businessman Kwek Long Bong for $325 million; and Time Warner Inc.'s purchase of Cablevision Industries for $2.2 billion.

The Decline of LBOs—Those "Internal" Mergers

Another difference in the new M&A variety is the decline of the leveraged buyout, the steamrolling, financial vehicle through which "internal mergers" became the big, top management ploy of the 1980s. Funded mostly through the use of junk bonds, LBOs toppled in number. In 1989, they totaled $51 billion in value or about 11 percent of the total value of all mergers. By 1993, they had dropped to $12 billion or 3 percent of the whole pie.

But don't count LBOs out. There's something infinitely interesting—visceral?—about a senior manager being able to buy the very company he or she works for along with some colleagues for 10 percent or less down (even by rolling over the stock purchases the company has helped the manager to buy) and having it all funded by some venture bankers, investment bankers, just plain banks, insurance companies and/or pension funds. It's a form of financial entrepreneurism that became so endemic to the American economy in the 1980s that the after-taste lingers on among many American business executives.

As it is, it's just waiting for the right people and the right situation. The Blackstone Group, one of the smaller but most dynamic New York investment banking houses, has created a separate fund of more than $600 million and more recently raised a new fund of almost double that for the purpose of funding LBOs and other takeover vehicles. The funds consist of committed capital from investors such as pension funds, banks, insurance companies and even well-heeled individuals.

Yet, the strictly financial takeover men have basically dropped out of the picture because of the descent of junk bonds and the reluctance of banks to participate in strictly financial acquisitions. With takeover prices jumping, the values to be paid are soaring too high to make sense to the LBO fund providers, unless the LBO is sound from a strategic sense. But don't let anyone tell you that LBOs are stone dead—they're just waiting.

But is it proper for, say, a chief executive and close associates to quietly set about acquiring a company when they are serving as its official, fiduciary senior managers? It is a question that has always intrigued me for several reasons. First, if we accept that inside relationship without quibbling, it means that insiders have the edge and the consent on doing something that they would quickly fire underlings for. Second, how can the Securities and Exchange Commission allow it and why haven't lawyers on the side of other, outside bidders taken a strong stand on what is obviously a discriminatory situation?

I am reminded of some candid comments that Edward Finkelstein, the former chairman of R.H. Macy, made to me in the late 1980s as he narrated the events in which he took the lead to buy that century-old company and take it private.

"I saw things happening in the retail business that could affect us... It was apparent to me that any undervalued company—most big retailers are undervalued—was open game for any company with money...I went through all the possibilities—buying back Macy stock, leaving my job and making a bid for the company from the outside, and so on. But none of these seemed to do what I wanted. I decided to do the toughest thing of all, a leveraged buyout," he said. It would be the toughest, he implied, because he would be investing his own money and that of his colleagues and risking it all.

"Why? We were losing people," he went on. "We were too short-term oriented. A month, two, or even a quarter doesn't matter much in our type of business. It takes a couple of years. I knew, too, that our down year of 1985 had to be improved and we could only do it by concentrating on our business, offering incentive to our best people so that they could work harder. We found that an executive who put in, say, $70,000—which he could get by cashing in his Macy stock and rolling it over to pay his share—could, if our calculations were right, build it into $3.5 million to $4 million if he worked hard and could wait it out.

"And we could get about 350 people into it ... and we could create some dilution so that more lower-rank executives could get involved. For $17,500, they could get as much as $1.5 million..."

Bottom-line? They all lost their shirts. Macy's, with the added poor judgment of acquiring two other retail chains, was unable to cope with more than $4 billion in debt, went into voluntary bankruptcy and in late 1994 was acquired by its arch rival, Federated Department Stores.

Yet, it is certain that the itch that energized Ed Finkelstein still resides under the skin of lots of top senior executives in every American industry today. So, while one of the major differences in current mergers is the decline of the leveraged buyout and its replacement by the merger from without, that could be just a temporary matter.

Using More Cash or Stock Versus Bonds or Notes

Another big difference, implied in the decline of junk bonds, is the use of stock and/or cash in the new consolidations as opposed to primary use of bonds or notes. After several years of belt-tightening, curtailed capital expenditures and downsizing, many companies have accumulated considerable cash. In addition, since the stock market crash of October 1987, many corporations have taken advantage of the low prices in their stocks to accumulate their own shares. Hence, when bitten by the acquisition bug, they have both the cash and the securities to fund the deal.

How is all this affecting the prices that merger-makers find themselves compelled to pay? They have had to pay through the nose, but don't feel too sorry for them. It's not their money because it comes from the banks, insurance companies or pension funds that themselves stand to gain much from the investment. Even though there are fewer $1 billion-plus deals, the prices of the big ones that are being consummated are inflated because of the strategic foundations of the deal which tend to raise the expectations of the selling company. The booming stock market also contributes its share of the fatter price tags. But implicit in this is the fact that the stock market and the M&A community tend to operate in conflict with each other. High stock values build an elevated base on which to bid for a company, creating difficulties for merger brokers so that under ordinary circumstances Wall Street and the M&A community can hardly work in tandem. But when the stock market falls, the merger arena gets busy.

Case in point: the peak period in mergers was triggered by Black Monday in October 1987 when many stocks plunged 50 percent and more. From 1987 through 1990—soaring most in 1989, as we have already said—mergers were rampant. Their decline in 1991 and 1992 is generally attributed to the slack in the domestic economy. The pervading cliché is that "Mergers boom in bad times because businesses are in trouble and are vulnerable and decline when the economy improves because the companies are more self-sufficient."

Is that always true? We shall view it from different standpoints throughout this book. So why are there more M&A transactions these days than back in the good, old year of 1989? Strategic reasons, for one thing. These denote efforts by companies to increase market share in the same industry, to enter related ones or obtain a rival's business, all through mergers or acquisitions. Also the fact is that many American companies are in the midst of recycling themselves from a severe recession, loss of markets to foreign countries and high operating costs. Moreover, the greater dollar volume of many M&As stems from the resurgence of the economy.

So a company becomes a "play." Once it does find itself in "play," meaning that it has emerged as an acquisition target, it soon dawns on its management that it had better play a friendly hand with one of its suitors. If not, the company may wind up with one not so attractive or welcome. It marks the onset of a delicate power game.

For its part, the company that puts another into "play" by offering to buy it quickly knows, or learns, that a company in "play" is one in rapid movement. Delay in cementing a deal can be painful, non-productive and ultimately defeating. But the real onus is on the target company, not the attacker, because the "play" label is a stubbornly sticky one, affecting the firm's stability long after the attacker goes home.

A Batch of "Plays" That Became Big Deals

When *The New York Times* made its $1 billion-plus offer for *The Boston Globe*, I am told that the *Times* had been interested in this for some time but had continued to hold off "until the economy improved." But when word started filtering through that another media chain might be making eyes at the *Globe*, the *Times* decided it had to move.

When the General Electric Capital Corporation came knocking at the door of Kemper Insurance, no one could have been less interested in a corporate combination than Kemper's board. But when the directors saw that GECC was determined and might raise the bid and go direct to the shareholders, Kemper's board saw that it had to be realistic. And so a deal was worked out for a higher price with another company.

When Paramount Communications was first approached by Viacom, the Paramount board was not particularly interested, even though there were good feelings between its management and that of Viacom. But when Barry Diller, the chairman of QVC Network, came riding over the horizon with a higher deal and a bidding war was touched off, Paramount knew the joys and terrors of being "in play." A deal with Viacom was arranged.

It is interesting that Paramount was then involved in its own acquisition transaction, that of buying an important chunk of Macmillan, Inc., a rival publisher. How often does a company that is hotly involved in buying another suddenly find that it itself has become a takeover pigeon? Paramount is hardly the first or the last to experience that sort of turnabout situation. Does that mean that any company must look over its shoulder all the time so that it doesn't fall into the sort of situation where the hawk turns out to be the pigeon? Absolutely.

But perhaps no other field has become so strategically merger-acquisition minded in recent months as the health-care industry. Scrambling to prepare itself for eventual passage of a national health-care program fostered by President Bill Clinton and his wife, Hillary, the major pharmaceuticals companies have been snapping up service operations in their field like never before.

In the most recent transaction, Eli Lilly & Company paid $4 billion in cash to acquire McKesson Corporation's PCS Health Systems Inc., the nation's largest pharmacy benefits management company. PCS provides prescription and managed care services for almost 50 million people, with annual spending for pharmaceutical products exceeding $6 billion. That figure was expected to grow to $9 billion by the end of McKesson's fiscal year on March 31, 1995.

Earlier, Merck & Company, the world's largest drug producer, bought Medco Containment Services, Inc., a big medical products distributor, for $6.6 billion. And SmithKline Beecham PLC acquired United Healthcare Corporation's Diversified Pharmaceutical Services for $2.2 billion. All three purchases have the common goal of offering the buyers a stronger position in which to compete in the exploding health-care field. And for the selling company, as McKesson's chairman and chief executive officer, Alan Seelenfreund, put it, the benefits of being acquired by a well-heeled parent will yield much the same benefit.

"The movement toward more aggressive managed care and the recent acquisition of several other prescription benefit managers by pharmaceutical manufacturers has made the business much more competitive," said Seelenfreund in the merger statement. "PCS is now competing against companies with substantially greater clinical resources, detail forces, physician relationships, disease state management protocols and research and development budgets. In the light of this changed environment and the offer from Lilly," he said, "we believe that this transaction represents the best opportunity to maximize shareholder value."

"Maximizing shareholder value" translates easily. It means a better bottom line, the maintenance and possible increase in the dividend and a better market value because the competitive stance of both seller and buyer has been enhanced. Only it usually doesn't happen that way. The seller's stock goes up; the buyer's goes down. Dividends go different ways; and stock values vary. Of course, all that isn't permanent but the effects last a while. They last long enough to be a frequent source of annoyance, frustration, and even regret among the shareholders of the buying company. On the other hand, the benefits of acquisitions can be a source of great joy when they do materialize to those who made the deal.

Professor Lipsey's View: Mergers DO Help

If business consolidations of the 1990s are clearly different from their earlier counterparts, is there also a difference in their benefits to the American society and the American economy? In other words, if "conglomeritis," leveraged buyouts and junk bonds were equated with "questionable" or "bad," are strategic mergers bought with the more solid mettle of cash or stock now viewed as "unquestionable," "productive" and "good"?

In doing research for my earlier book on mergers, I found that almost all academics frowned on mergers as unproductive, very disruptive for people, and monopolistic. Not so this time, as I learned on interviewing several economics professors. At most, they think that mergers help to straighten out an economy. At worst, they tend to equivocate on the morality.

Robert E. Lipsey of Queens College, the City University of New York, is also a research associate of the respected National Bureau of Economic Research. Here's what he said in a widely-ranging discussion:

"Economists now feel that mergers bring efficiency and productivity benefits in that less efficient firms are taken over by more efficient ones. So, on the whole, there should be some improvement."

"But there could be a loss of competition, a loss to the country because of the diminished dynamism of competition," he added. "Personally, I don't think anyone can say for certain that today's mergers are all good or all bad. It depends upon conditions in an industry. In Sweden, firms taken over were mostly in trouble. But in the United States, the evidence is contradictory. American firms taken over by foreign companies were lame ducks so that, in that sense, those cases could lead to more competition, rather than less," said Professor Lipsey.

"In terms of academic study, most of the empirical literature shows that there are benefits from mergers except for a few academic observers who saw the conglomerate takeovers as mostly mistakes," he went on. "Yet, it is likewise true that in today's non-conglomerate mergers there is a loss of employment. That, however, isn't necessarily a bad sign for the country since it's widely perceived that many corporations grew overinflated in infrastructure and people. The bigger question is have we adequately taken care of the displaced people who had a large stake in the acquired company, many years of service and so on?"

Professor Lipsey said that employees generally emerged better from takeovers in Europe than in the U.S. which is a "faster-moving economy." But then he asked, "Have U.S. companies given employees too much—buying loyalty through continuous employment even when prolonging it may not have been realistic? If so, this may have long-term dangers for them. Yet we have suffered much less unemployment than European countries. There's an implicit irony in that in Europe. Because European managements have taken pains to make it hard to get rid of people, they have made it more difficult for young people to get those good jobs."

In the United States, Professor Lipsey said, the proliferation of mergers as well as the downsizing of American business has had a directly negative effect on employee loyalty. It's a fairly new phenomenon, he said, that the big American companies have offered less stable employment, particularly to white-collar personnel who have always felt very safe. "And it's possible that companies will have to revert somewhat to the former policy of more corporate paternalism."

One of the ironies of corporate takeovers is that financial companies seem to value corporations less when they remain intact than when they are in play, Professor Lipsey observed. Hence, the bidding on Kemper Insurance soared once General Electric Company made its initial bid. "Why is the target company suddenly worth more?" asked Professor Lipsey. "The financial markets see the takeover first as a way of improving the productivity of the acquired company and then as a vehicle to provide the benefits of the economy of scale. That's the plus side of the financial markets' scrutiny. The minus side is that if the merger is big enough in a particular industry, it could achieve enough monopolistic status to bring the government's scrutiny down on it with possibly punitive results."

Turning to chief executives' behavior, when faced by the likelihood of a takeover, most sink into a quandary on how to react. If the price is right, said Professor Lipsey, the chief executive will support it by insisting it is good for the shareholders. But it is probably also personally profitable, providing he or she keeps a cool head in the process, because the CEO may get more power as the ruling expert of the acquired company, as well as more income. This scenario, of course, does not always happen. Or the CEO may resist the unexpected bid. "It's not clear to me," the Professor said, "how independent a CEO can be in facing a merger offer. There are clear conflicts of interest."

In other words, one part of the CEO's head is personal, the other is fiduciary on behalf of the company and its shareholders. As I learned in some earlier merger confrontations, a CEO can remain steeped in dismay and indecision for days while the attacker skulks around the beleaguered camp and finds plenty of additional ways to further dig in around it. In one particular case, by the time the CEO rallied with a plan of defense, the attacker decided to up the bid and did so repeatedly until the company was won.

Asked "Why are people in general less vociferous in favor or against mergers than they used to be?" Professor Lipsey said, "I think people are less worried about mergers despite their dramatic size because they're more concerned nowadays about efficiency than they were 20 years ago. They worry that productivity alone isn't enough to withstand foreign competition but believe that quality and efficiency are more important. They're not even sure that the government should intervene on an antitrust basis as it did with IBM when the federal government nit-picked it some years ago. That's not to say that the government shouldn't intervene when a small number of big companies control a market. There is such a point where that is reached in various American industries.

"But would government action against a giant or several giants work against our competitive ability on the international front?" he asked. "For example, Boeing Aircraft is the dominant American aircraft manufacturer. But no one in the U.S. would want Boeing to be dismantled if it is to remain competitive against the European combination that makes the Airbus. Boeing always seems to be fighting for its life, so why kill it altogether?"

Are the Megadeal's Risks Manageable?

There's no question in my mind that the really big difference in present-day mergers is the huge size of some of the deals.

Irrespective of other factors—motivation of the principals, the type of financial backing employed, the intrinsic goal of the consolidations, the human factors and so on—it seems to me that the very marrow of the deals is the mega-amount of the dollars involved. In 1986, the $30 billion cost of the RJR Reynolds-Nabisco merger convinced many that the merger-acquisition binge had reached its dollar zenith. But, seven years later we contemplated with open mouths an even greater deal—the $33 billion, pending merger of Bell Atlantic and Tele-Communications Company, the huge cable-TV concern. It was potentially the biggest merger of all time, until Bell Atlantic decided to withdraw its offer when its stock values fell below a strategic level. But the original merger announcement not only immediately set tongues wagging on which top officer would survive—Raymond W. Smith, chief executive of Bell Atlantic or John C. Malone, president of Tele-Communications—but whether the federal government would allow a combination that would certainly be anticompetitive and whether this was not truly the one event that would transform America's telecommunications industry.

Oddly enough, after an initial "gee-whiz" type of reaction at the amount of money involved, little comment lingered over whether American business and its Mom 'n Pop shareholders weren't hocking their financial future for astronomical deals. And—now is the time to confess all—the idea came to me to pursue this track of thinking to its ultimate possibility.

Now I quickly grant that the amount of dollars involved in a business transaction isn't necessarily any indication of any underlying factors. After all, we can argue that annual inflation alone might cut enough of the fat from any deal to make it seem not so extreme. For example, $1 million in 1986 might be worth $1.3 million or $1.5 million today; $10 million in 1986 might be worth $12.5 million now, maybe more. And one could rationalize it further; the dollar has lost value internationally so that any foreign banks joining a lending syndicate might demand more than they would have a few years ago, changing the terms of the proposed deal. And so on.

But what I think a $33 billion deal really implies, especially one that combines one of the nation's biggest telephone companies and the country's largest cable operator, is that there are no longer any limits to business combinations in terms of money paid for them, or in size of companies, or the implicit assets that are involved. And, of course, this wide-open door also pertains to the merger's consequent effect on employees, suppliers and competition.

But, perhaps, I'm just an alarmist, filling a traditional function as the rambunctious journalist. At least that's what I may be judging by what Albert C. Sikes, former chairman of the Federal Communications Commission, said about the pending Bell Atlantic-Tele-Communications deal on October 15, 1993 in an Op-Ed article in the *New York Times* headlined, "Deal of the Century." He wrote that the merger might serve as "a catalyst to similar mega-mergers in the future," but he added, "The concern will be, of course, that such a merger is anticompetitive. I, for one, speaking as a former FCC commissioner, think that the merger's promises outweigh its risks. And I think the risks are manageable. The merger partners claim the deal is in fact pro-competitive, and this seems right. Thanks in part to rapid technological progress, the twin monopolies of cable TV and telephone service are becoming more and more vulnerable to competition. With this merger and others like it, the real competition will begin."

But, for all his seemingly total support, Sikes is candid enough to state that the merger could be against the public interest but will not be "unless the government falls asleep." He suggests that the government should not let these companies combine facilities in the same markets and should encourage them "to confront the monopolies in each other's industries." At the same time, he says, the two merger partners should push Washington's leadership to "change badly outdated laws."

Will the federal government step in and force the suggested changes? Will it also agree to "change badly outdated laws"? At this writing, not yet. So at this stage it appears, almost anything goes. That's one of the big changes today.

chapter 2

When the Urge to Merge Becomes the Zest to Divest

Picture this scenario:

Starting life as a single, orange orchard in Grove City, California in 1955, Continental Citrus Growers thrived from the intensive efforts of Smilin' Bill Hills. The former World War II artilleryman held on to his Army discharge money, added to it by working in the orange groves and bought the nearby Grove City orchard. Because he was a very pragmatic and hard-working grower, he soon was able to buy another orchard, then a third, and a fourth. By 1960, he owned more than a dozen orchards. Eventually, Bill shipped more crates of oranges than just about anyone else in California.

Smilin' Bill also caught the Wall Street bug. In fact, the revenues he got from taking his company public enabled him to buy not only more orchards but other kinds of farms, too. He decided to build a conglomerate. He bought a large, Southern California shipyard. Within the next three years, he bought two more shipbuilding companies; two shopping centers; a big chunk of the state's fish-packing industry; a medium-sized metal fabricating business and one of the most established, smaller aircraft makers. He used the same method that he did in selecting oranges to ship. If it looked good and it felt good, it was good. In less than 20 years, he built a $2.5 billion grab-bag of businesses. Much admired, he made the cover of *Fortune* magazine and was profiled also in both *Business Week* and *Forbes. Forbes* also listed him in the second-tier of America's richest men. Although he had never finished high school, Smilin' Bill Hills also received several honorary degrees from leading Western universities.

To reflect its true nature, Continental Citrus Growers changed its name to Continental Industries. Then one day he received a message that most of his acquisitions were not operating as well as expected. In 1985, after Smilin' Bill suffered his first heart-attack, his investment bankers and attorneys presented him with a grand plan to restructure his business and divest everything he had but the original one or two orchards. When he was down to his last orchard in 1990 he died with a happy smile on his face. It was the gratified expression of someone who had gone far but had come home to his simple beginnings. Why else do you think they called him Smilin' Bill? Well it's a good story.

Why the Collectors of Companies Began to Shed Them

The rush to divest collections of heterogeneous holdings became one of the big business games of the 1980s. In more than one case, like that of the fictional Smilin' Bill Hills, a simple rustic developed in a single generation into a typical American wheeler-dealer. It represented one of those great American folk-tales. But in the mid-1980s, the wheel began turning the other way and many of these company collectors rushed to sell what they had accumulated. The plain fact is that conglomerates were pretty much a failure. They didn't deliver anything like the synergism, profits, or efficiencies they had promised.

Why? Why, in fact, did the bulk of the Fortune 500 companies begin shedding many of their once-beloved entities, for which they had shelled out many hundreds of millions of dollars only a few years earlier?

There were three reasons. One, in a lot of cases, the headquarters management found that it couldn't digest all the companies it had bought because its members just didn't know enough and the divisional managements they had inherited or hired weren't delivering. Two, conglomerate stocks were selling at less than the value of their parts. Three—most important—the core idea of the conglomerate philosophy, that diversity was a better hedge than being in just one or two industries, was proving fallacious under the nasty whip of the economic recession of the late 1980s and early 1990s.

And there was another, irritating reason. As the merged RJR-Nabisco learned to its dismay, the large institutional investors (and many smaller ones) always seemed to value companies not for their stable of companies but for their original or largest unit. Hence, RJR-Nabisco's new, private owners learned that their company was still seen as basically a tobacco company, not as the diversified owner of many well-known food lines as well. These had been brought into the fold through the marriage of Nabisco, the giant, packaged foods maker, which itself had earlier acquired Standard Brands, another big foods producer. So the merger idea did not pay off. The stock market merely chalked up RJR-Nabisco as a tobacco stock and saw it with "iffy" prospects in view of the cancer scare and the pressure against the effect of secondary smoke.

There are many examples of breaking up conglomerates but let's examine just a few.

A Gallery of Deconglomerates

- *Ethyl Corporation.* In 1973, when the federal government said that tetraethyl lead, the antiknock element in gasoline, was hazardous to consumers and that its production be discontinued, Ethyl Corporation, the country's leading antiknock product maker, complied and bought its way into plastics, aluminum, coal, specialty chemicals, pharmaceuticals and even insurance. But the stock market, after first approving the conglomerate, had a change of heart and showed it in the lowered value of Ethyl's stock. So the Gottwald family, Ethyl's largest shareholders, decided to "undiversify."

First, Floyd and Bruce Gottwald, the family's senior members, convinced the board to spin off Tredegar Industries, the aluminum, plastics and energy business, in 1989. Then in 1993 they spun off First Colony Insurance and in March 1994 they also launched Albemarle Chemicals on its own. The brothers had an ulterior motive, however, in breaking up the conglomerate. Each brother had two sons, so divesting four businesses would allow them to place one son over each, thus solving a potentially troubling family issue. And Ethyl now has returned to its old position as a petroleum additives company: back to its roots after many a fling.

- *B. F. Goodrich Company*. As imports caused competition in the automotive tire business to heat up, Goodrich sold its tire operation in 1986 to concentrate on the production of polyvinyl chloride, the waterproofing compound and insulating material that was the mainstay of its specialty chemicals business. In 1993 when the PVC market appeared to be maturing, Goodrich sold its PVC operation. But instead of concentrating on the other chemicals, Goodrich's CEO, John D. Ong, chose 1994 as the year to move into the aerospace business. Using the proceeds from the PVC sale, Ong bought the Cleveland Pneumatic Company, which makes landing-gear, and Rosemont Aerospace, producer of flight data sensors. The purchases were ill-timed for the aerospace industry was mired in a deep slump because of severe cutbacks by the government.

    Things took an unexpected turn. Geon, the PVC business Goodrich sold, has done well while the two, new aerospace subsidiaries have yet to show their true mettle. So Goodrich, one of America's pioneer tire producers, is now out of it, heavily involved in specialty chemicals and airplane parts and hoping that the aircraft industry will revive soon. The company's stock dropped to the mid-$40s, well down from $69, its recent high. Frequent reinvention seems to be the motto at Goodrich, not to mention some busy buying and selling.

- *Jostens Inc.* Sometimes, too much success can turn your head. This highly successful maker of school graduation products—class rings, yearbooks and class photos—had enjoyed an unbroken success record for more than three decades until its management began to worry in the 1980s because its annual earnings growth slowed to mid-single digits. What could be done to bring it up again? H. William Lurton, the longtime company chief executive, became enamored with the interactive, educational software business, otherwise known as "multimedia." And why not? Wasn't Jostens an expert in the educational field and weren't schools enthused about using computers and electronics to provide better teaching methods?

  So Jostens, very comfortable and at home in school rings, bought a 25 percent stake in Broderbund Software Company and in 1989 paid $65 million for the Education Systems Corporation. It was, to put it mildly, a disaster. At first successful, Jostens' electronic fling turned very sticky when educators decided it was better to run software on a variety of computers than just on the special computers Jostens sold. Besides, there were additional Josten charges, such as $112,000 the initial year and $12,000 each year of the contract. And with school budgets everywhere going through the wringer, Jostens' product and service were just too costly. In 1993, Lurton left his job and a new chief executive began what remained into some semblance of reality.

- *Emerson Electric Corporation.* The watershed in this 100-year-old-plus company came in the mid-1980s when a big industrial customer told CEO Charles Knight that it could pay $10 less per compressor by buying it in Brazil rather than from Emerson in St. Louis. Investigation showed Knight that the Brazilian supplier wasn't just benefiting from cheap labor but had built a new plant and was buying steel for 25 percent less than he was. Further checking confirmed this from other foreign suppliers. Knight realized that he had to cut costs, shift plants to lower cost areas of the country and get rid of diversified businesses that Emerson had accumulated to shore up its static industrial business and which may have caused Knight and his senior people to be diverted from their main business.

So out went a number of construction and defense subsidiaries, a Weed Eater gardening tool company and others. Did the divesting make the difference? Well, as Knight found out, not really, but it allowed him to clear his head and those of his top team so that they could plan more clearly how to make a profit. The horizon now looks much brighter so that Emerson has embarked on a new but wiser diversification program more related to its core business.

- *Eastman Kodak Company.* Talk about the ironies of conglomerates and their subsequent contortions to divest, what about a case where a company diversifies primarily to get revenge on a competitor who invaded its turf? That's what happened to the much respected Kodak. In 1988, Kodak paid $5.1 billion for the Sterling Drug Company in a diversification plan to counter the inroads of Fuji, the Japanese film maker, which had mounted a big U.S. campaign on behalf of its brand of film. Kodak really believed that its purchase of such Sterling brands as the Lysol line of cleaners, Mop & Glo cleaner, Resolve carpet cleaners, Chubbs Baby Wipes and Wet Ones moist towelettes would strengthen its business and indirectly help it battle Fuji.

But in mid-1994, Kodak's new chairman, George M.C. Fisher, who had replaced the ousted Kay R. Whitmore the previous December, decided that too much diversity was hurting the company. He announced that Kodak would sell everything not related to photography and electronic imaging. And the company proceeded to do just that in four major moves over a four-month period. It sold its over-the-counter pharmaceuticals business to SmithKline Beecham, the British pharmaceuticals giant, for $2.93 billion; its prescription drug division was sold to Sanofi, a French drug firm, for $1.7 billion; the diagnostics business went to Johnson & Johnson for more than $1 billion and its household products division was sold to Reckitt & Colman PLC., a British household and food products company, for $1.55 billion.

Other Kodak non-photography operations were also put on the block. Obviously, if Kodak ended its big diversification fling in less than six years, it was a bad move to begin with.

The Results of Failing to Know Other Businesses

There may be some diehards who insist it isn't so, but it's hard to deny the fact that conglomerates were both structurally and strategically ill-conceived. This basic problem was covered over by most of the "highly confident" letters signed and distributed by almost all the principal investment bankers to build credibility for conglomerate mergers that would eventually bring big dollars flowing into their coffers. But aside from the reasons I cited earlier—management inability to digest the acquisitions, insufficient research, weak divisional managements—it's likely that the company that accumulated from eight to 30 divisions in different fields simply refused to understand that each industry has a different set of economics that needs close attention and overseeing by senior management.

For example, for years shopping mall developers insisted that they could operate department stores better than those which were their tenants and never quite delivered the degree of return and revenues that the developers thought they should. So three of them bought some well-known retail chains. But Robert Campeau, the Canadian developer, failed and was finally routed by Federated Department Stores; A. Alfred Taubman, the dynamic mall owner, acquired both Woodward & Lothrop in Washington, D.C. and the John Wanamaker stores in Philadelphia and then had to put them into voluntary bankruptcy. And the Crown American Corporation, a Johnstown, Pennsylvania-based developer, bought the Hess's Inc. chain in Allentown, Pennsylvania, increased the number of stores from 17 to 70 and then closed them all.

No less bright were the results achieved by such ambitious conglomerates as ITT Corporation; Leasco Data Processing Corporation; Ling-Temco-Vought; Northwest Industries, and even General Motors Corporation. All found that most of the companies they had bought in the flush of corporate ambition and personal gratification were not yielding the expected results. Investors and shareholders were complaining, and the company directors were losing patience.

In 1984, General Motors paid a hefty $2.5 billion to Ross Perot for Electronic Data Systems, the Plano, Texas computer-services company which he had founded. Even after the rambunctious Perot left the GM board and ceased his counsel on EDS, GM was having second thoughts about the computer business, particularly the EDS speciality of "outsourcing," which handles and manages the data centers for large companies. GM thought that acquiring EDS might work some wonders by combining a major industrial business with a corps of computer experts. But that synergy failed to develop; so in May 1994, GM put EDS up for sale. And, sure enough, Sprint Corporation, the third-largest telephone company, bit and a merger seemed to be in the offing that would create a $20 billion information monolith. Only it didn't happen. and the reasons and the interplay are worth noting.

The two sides, it seemed, couldn't agree on which would be more equal. On May 16, 1994, EDS and Sprint had announced that they had agreed to a "merger of equals." Eleven days later, in a shift that was shocking to EDS management, Sprint brass asked for a higher exchange rate of 1.3 shares in the new company that Sprint would get instead of the initially agreed 1.1 shares. Then the letters began. On June 1, Lester M. Alberthal, Jr., EDS's CEO, and John F. Smith, Jr., GM's chairman, wrote a "Dear Bill" letter to William T. Esrey, Sprint's CEO, charging that the new demand "ignored the very principles of a merger of equals."

"Dear Jack and Les," Esrey responded on June 3, observing that basing an exchange ratio on current market prices "would be naive." Moreover he said that relative market prices did not reflect the "potential adverse impact" on EDS's trading price as a result of "nonpublic information that has come to our attention." What was that? demanded EDS. This mysterious reference which implied wrongdoing on the part of EDS was not explained by Sprint. And it was roundly denied by EDS. It also spelled the end, for the time being, at least, of the eagerness of GM to get rid of its ill-judged acquisition and of EDS's management to shed itself of an uncomfortable and unproductive ownership. As in many conglomerate or otherwise diversified M&A's, the GM-EDS merger was one that was not right from the outset.

In a variation on breaking up conglomerates, some major corporations have seriously studied the concept of splitting significant divisions away from the rest of the company, either because there have been inherent problems in the spinoff target that have needed particular attention or because the stock market would grant a premium for the values of the separate companies rather than for the total. A dramatic example is the Philip Morris Companies, the nation's biggest producer of cigarettes, which early in 1994 said it was considering a spinoff of its tobacco business. This would leave its other business of food and beer as one company and tobacco as another.

The pressure in Congress against tobacco producers and the industry's denial that cigarette smoking is addictive were undoubtedly behind the thought of spinoff. But some concern about how that debate might affect the company's total stock was surely involved as well. Philip Morris' tobacco revenues in 1993 were vast, $15.7 billion of which $10.2 billion were domestic sales. Foreign sales were up 15 percent that year while domestic sales dropped almost as much in percentage.

Does it prove that tobacco, food, beer, etc., just don't mix? Or that each brings a business separate problems? Or that companies that just get too big will have troubles anyway, especially if the focus has to be spread on a range of different disciplines? My guess is that all three questions deserve a definite "yes."

The Role of Conglomerates Recycling America

If conglomerates were largely ill-conceived and mostly failed, where do they fit into the fabric of modern American business history?

A decade after the end of World War II, the U.S. had completed a full turnaround from war to peace to prosperity. Conventionally structured companies based around one, two or even three products and services were running up against limited growth potential. Hundreds of new, startup companies were already maturing by 1955 or were stymied by lack of capital or financing for expansion. Brokered by Wall Street and by investment bankers who saw great market-share growth in them, inter-industry mergers sprouted, grew and then mushroomed.

Before it was even widely perceived, big, single-industry companies were snapping up smaller- and medium-sized businesses. Quite suddenly, bucolic towns and calm cities were visited by squads of big company representatives, brandishing big dollars and promising great times ahead. Some of the buyers fought with one another over a particularly toothsome acquisition, which helped to elevate the offering price. Many of the transactions began with a hostile approach from the buyer but concluded with smiles on both ends, reflecting agreement on a new price and in many cases certain emoluments such as outright gifts and assurances of good, post-merger perks.

The buying binge by such companies as ITT, Gulf & Western, Ling-Temco-Vought, IC Industries and Cargill Inc. raised concern at the regulatory agencies, Congress and the White House. Strictures were put into effect on both vertical and horizontal mergers that tended to create an antitrust situation. These "merger enforcement policy statements" covered vertical mergers in the cement industry, geographic market extension mergers in food distribution, and product extension mergers in dairy processing and grocery products manufacturing. By taking a strong stand when toughness was needed, the Feds felt that they could avoid needless litigation since business would already know or suspect what types of mergers were most likely to be challenged. This, however, required a sharp lookout and prompt action by the government on those mergers that violated the policy embodied in the enforcement statements. This placed a special spotlight on the Federal Trade Commission which was obligated to oversee any antitrust problems in consumer-oriented industries. In the late 1960s, the FTC fell down on the job in connection with food retailing so that a record number of takeovers occurred in the supermarket industry.

In 1969 and 1970, the government rallied and stiffened its enforcement policy. The Justice Department declared its intention to challenge all large conglomerate mergers among the top 200 industrial corporations. Justice, in other words, would eagerly look into any acquisition of a leading company by any of the top 200, or any conglomerate merger that created "substantial opportunities for reciprocity." It was a shocker for ambitious, large companies, the investment banking community and that growing part of the legal profession that had zeroed in on mergers and acquisitions.

Led by hard-charging Richard W. McLaren, Assistant Attorney General in charge of the antitrust division (within his first seven months he had already become the biggest trust-buster since President Theodore Roosevelt), Justice challenged manufacturing and mining mergers representing 27 percent of the assets of all large mergers attempted or consummated in 1969. This served to dampen much of the ardor of conglomerate mergers starting in 1970. From 1968 to 1970, there were an average 174 mergers per year, but during 1971 and 1972 the annual average dropped to 88 a year, or by 51 percent.

But that was it for a while. Justice turned its attention elsewhere. Conglomerate mergers picked up again. The Celler-Kefauver Act, which restrained antitrust movement, had been in effect since 1951, but clearly there was confusion more than a quarter-century later about how to handle conglomerate mergers because of their size and the intrinsic, entrepreneurial nature of the national economy. Some of this doubt was expressed by Willard F. Mueller, chief economist of the FTC in his December 1978 study of the Celler-Kefauver Act:

"... Inaction without respect to conglomerate mergers is a kind of action, a sanctioning of the status quo in the name of agnosticism because our knowledge is incomplete. In balancing the probable costs of inaction, a policy of wait and see, against the probable costs of action that subsequent events may prove unwarranted, the latter is the wiser course. For should a course of action prove later to have sacrificed some economic efficiency, the matter can be righted by changing policy. On the other hand, should we pursue a policy of inaction, an essentially laissez-faire attitude toward conglomerate mergers, there is a high probability that the economy will become centralized in a fashion that cannot be reversed."

Nonetheless, the government's now-heavy, now-light hand soon became unnecessary. By the mid- and late-1960s the conglomerates were self-correcting and self-destructing. The dazzling variety of being in as many as a dozen or more industries was turning into a drain and a distraction for senior managers. They were also disappointed by the paltry returns they were getting from many of the acquisitions. By 1972, many of those acquired companies were cast loose and faced the challenge of survival or extinction.

Enter the leveraged buyout. It became the financial vehicle of the decade-plus, allowing a senior management group to take its company private by paying the shareholders a premium over the market price. The whole transaction was financed by banks and financial institutions which obtained equity ownership in the new company, as well as other fees. Senior executives liked this system because they only had to put up about 10 percent of the money, sometimes less. There was the added attraction that the tax laws allowed companies in LBOs to deduct depreciation of plant and equipment from their taxes. Of course, the lenders walked away with most of the company. But the eventual goal was to build up the company so that when it was brought public again the senior management investors would make a bundle. It became one of the most popular forms of financial entrepreneurism, even though ultimately most of the LBOs did not pay off and small shareholders of the original company could only look back with regret on their captive sellout.

Then came junk bonds. Their relationship with mergers began in 1983. Low-rated, high-yield bonds were just right for companies that didn't have enough cash flow to rate regular financing. These companies could buy, do an LBO, divest, merge or do any sort of financial transaction with junk bonds. Risk-takers loved them: the junk bonds paid between 13 and 15 percent interest whereas the high-rated bonds paid only 10 percent. The risk of default was high and some of Wall Street's straight-arrow investment houses refused to deal in them.

But others did. Michael Milken of Drexel Burnham Lambert dealt in them to the extent of many billions of dollars worth, as did others. And he probably would have continued to deal in them if he hadn't been tagged later for alleged insider trading and sent to prison. But whatever wrong Milken did, he helped many smaller companies to finance their growth when the establishment banking system looked the other way.

So where do conglomerates fit into our business history? They were the conduit through which American business recycled itself for better or worse. As the economy swelled with the startups of thousands of companies, many lost their *raison d'etre* through the rise of technology, the massive flow of imports or simple bad management. They were the conglomerators' meat. But these captive companies were chewed up by the financial meat-grinder. Thousands and thousands of people lost their jobs, most of them unable to find a position that paid the money they were making or which required anything near their special skills. In my opinion, the rise and fall of conglomerates was one of the dark chapters in American business but it was probably inevitable.

But now we face a more wholesome version of the conglomerate—one that holds some real promise for the future.

chapter 3

The Strategic Merger

The Barry Diller Epic

Few strategists have been so annoyed, harassed and frustrated in recent years as Barry Diller. Brilliant and mercurial, the hard-driving Diller reached high and fell hard.

Twice in 1994, the chairman and chief executive of QVC Inc., the home shopping network, marched to the altar only to have the bride slip away. A hyperambitious man intent on making his mark in a big way, he drew his sights on Paramount Communications in a prolonged, six-month war only to be outbid in February by Viacom Inc. Then in June, in his second move, he made a deal with Laurence Tisch, the chairman of CBS Inc., the top-rated television network, to merge CBS and QVC with Diller running CBS and owning a 3 percent stake.

Only it wasn't a deal. Comcast Inc. a cable television company which had its own big stake in QVC and had never warmed to the merger with CBS, suddenly made an offer in

July of $2.2 billion, or $44 per share, for the 84 percent of QVC's stock that it didn't own. Not only did the $44 a share exceed the $38 a share QVC would get from its merger with CBS, but the higher offer also meant that QVC would be unable to pursue its quest of CBS. For Diller, the timing of the turn-about couldn't have been more terrible.

The saga of Barry Diller, while itself abortive, reflects the great trend in the 1990s to extend a company's reach, scope and growth through merging with a company in similar or related fields. Although the merger of the industry-leading QVC with the third-ranking Comcast would have widely expanded QVC's market, Diller's real strategy was to combine his shopping network with the news-and-entertainment might of CBS. But the Comcast initiative was also embarrassing to CBS because it left the big network floundering and exposed, a deserted bride, so to speak, and not particularly comfortable whether a new suitor appeared or not.

Up till then, Diller seemed to have led a charmed life, often by defying the odds and then having them work in his favor. He began a spectacular career at ABC television in 1967 as a programming executive. Based on such coups as his innovative ideas of mini-series and television movies, within two years he was promoted to head of programming at ABC-TV. But he was ready for bigger things, Hollywood in particular. In 1974, Paramount Pictures named him chairman and he quickly moved into producing exciting products for both movie theaters and television. Two of his biggest revenue makers were the movies. "Raiders of the Lost Ark" and "Star Trek" and he also scored with such television hits as "Happy Days" and "Laverne and Shirley."

In 1974, that first year at Paramount, he also obtained the television rights to Alex Haley's book, "Roots." The mini-series of that story of black history, which drew record audiences and top ratings, was one of the most dramatic successes that TV broadcasting has ever enjoyed. Even reruns were avidly watched by the public. And Barry Diller, who had been looking for something distinctive to make his mark, had finally found it. Because of his ABC success, he moved to Twentieth-Century Fox in 1984 as its chairman and chief executive officer. The

Australian publisher-financier, Rupert Murdoch, who bought Twentieth-Century Fox, gave Diller a go-ahead to start a fourth television network.

Throwing himself into what was at best a very difficult assignment, Diller signed comedienne Joan Rivers to "The Late Show," competing with the firmly entrenched Johnny Carson talk show on National Broadcasting. The show drew mixed ratings as did most of Fox's presentations. In its first two fiscal years Murdoch's deep pockets kept Fox alive as it lost a total $136 million. But in 1989, the third year, when Diller introduced the first telecast of "The Simpsons," the caustic, animated family saga, the network finally caught on and earned its first profit.

It was—or should have been—another spectacular success for Diller. But he was beyond that. Diller now needed to run his own show. At that point, he made his biggest and most enigmatic career move. He jumped Fox in 1992 to become chairman and CEO of QVC. Its eager board made him a partner and the beneficiary of a lavish remuneration package. The jump into home shopping from news, programming and entertainment surprised many Diller watchers, friends and enemies. But quickly he granted interviews that revealed a profound belief in the future of buying all manner of merchandise via the television set, computer and telephone. To listen to Barry, one would easily have thought that stores were going out of business rather than that home shopping was still only a merchandising infant representing well under 3 percent of total consumer purchases in the country.

Then came the unsuccessful bid for Paramount. Diller lost out on the bidding and walked away, a seemingly bitter and disappointed man. But he was hardly through. He heard that Larry Tisch might want to sell his big stake in CBS, that the hotel-insurance-theater owner might be losing interest in the demanding business of national television. CBS was having its problems. Fox had recently wrested eight affiliate CBS stations and had successfully bid for the games of the National Football League which CBS had carried for years. Diller knew Larry. Tisch was a conglomerate builder of old, who, with his brother, Preston Robert, had parlayed a tiny, resort hotel into a giant, diversified, multi-billion dollar company. But some felt that he was spreading himself too thin.

When Diller called, Tisch was ready. He liked and admired Diller, knowing that Barry was an achiever who might even rank at his level. But Diller, who was ordinarily so facile and charming in smoothing over obstacles, had made one slight error. He neglected to inform the Robertses who controlled 16 percent of QVC. It was an error that Diller will surely never forget.

Ralph Roberts, 74, and Brian, 35, were angry that Diller, whom they had personally brought over from Fox, had literally stabbed them in the back with his CBS merger initiative. When Diller had had his problems with Martin Davis, the parent company chief executive at Paramount, Ralph Roberts had personally inserted himself into the battle, telling the media, investors and everyone what a talent Barry was. But, when all was said and done, the real rub was economics. The merger with CBS would have cut Comcast's stake in QVC from its approximate 16 percent to less than 5 percent. The Robertses could have walked away from the deal that they didn't like with many millions of dollars. But their influence in the merged CBS-QVC and particularly in the latter would have been minimal.

I have gone into detail about Barry Diller because it seems to me after reporting on many mergers and acquisitions that there is always one individual who puts them together, particularly if they are strategic mergers. Investment bankers can do all the spadework; pension fund officers and insurance company CEOs can offer their financial support but it all comes down to one person who is pumping the gas pedal hard. If he or she doesn't, there's no deal.

Health-Care M&As Pace the Whole Trend

Perhaps no field has been as heated up by merger fever as the health-care industry. All have been strategic mergers. Call it a healthy dose of opportunity recognition whether it's a pharmaceuticals company wanting to get into the managed-care business or a life-insurer eager to join health-insurance business. Or consider some mind-boggling combinations like the maker of Advil and Anacin painkillers and oral contraceptives (American Home Products Company) buying its way (however hostile) into the vitamins, minerals and pesticides and weed-killer business (American Cyanamid).

American Home Products had to ante up another $500 million for a total $10 billion deal when Cyanamid's board insisted on playing hard-to-get. But what will it do with the vanquished company's pesticide and week-killer entities? We dare not mention its own heavy plate which includes Preparation H., Robitussin, Chap Stick, Chef Boyardee and Gulden's mustard.

Pushed by President Clinton's proposed health-care bill, insurance companies kept the M&A community hopping in both 1993 and 1994. In June of 1994, Travelers Companies and Metropolitan Life Insurance Company merged their health-coverage operations in a $1 billion transaction that would become the country's biggest health-insurer. Between its premiums and fees to be paid, MetLife/Travelers would have revenues of over $17.6 billion against the rest of the pack consisting of Cigna with $16.5 billion, Aetna Insurance with $15.3 billion and Prudential with $10.6 billion.

But more significant than size was the implicit strategy. Both MetLife and Travelers were in one big step moving out of the business of standard indemnity insurance in which they merely pay medical bills when received; now they were trying to switch the insured customers into the managed-care business like HMOs, medical plans and the like. Of course, it was merely preparing for the health-care blitz which would be ignited by a new national health program. And hadn't the Clinton administration publicly suggested mergers as a means of bringing down costs in the health-care field and preparing for the eventual passage of the legislation?

There were mutual arrangements of various mutations. The largest for-profit hospital company, Columbia/HCA Healthcare, bought the Medical Care America, the largest chain of surgery centers, for a total cost of $1.08 billion. Another hospital deal involved New York Hospital's regional alliance with seven other non-profit hospitals, two nursing homes and four walk-in clinics, with the unusual goal of sending their toughest cases to New York Hospital. HMOs, too, combined. Two California HMOs—FHP International and Takecare—merged to cover 1.6 million people in eight western states.

Physician groups were merging, too. A 200-physician Mullikin Medical Enterprises in Southern California bought the practices of a number of other California medical groups. Its goal is to cut costs and get lower charges from area hospitals through the clout of increased size.

Highly specialized producers were merging as well; for example, those who make heart valves and pacemakers. In June 1994, St. Jude Medical Inc., the St. Paul company that is the world's principal producer of heart valves, acquired the cardiac device operations of Siemens, A.G., the German electronics producer, for $500 million. Siemens Pacemaker, based in Los Angeles, is the world's second-largest pacemaker producer. For St. Jude, the move was a clear track to instant growth in a quickly growing field. But for its shareholders, the immediate news wasn't very positive. St. Jude simultaneously announced that it would cease paying dividends in order to pay for the acquisition. The company's CEO, Ronald Matricaria, however, took the long view. He said that his company was acquiring skilled sales and research staffs "in a $2 billion market segment with great growth potential."

Strategically, the emphasis in all these deals is to assure enough size, financial clout and customers to compete more effectively not only today but especially in the coming health-care reform. But while it all looks like a frenetic exercise, the immense opportunity and the scrambling for position ensure that it's probably only the beginning.

The Binge in Telecommunications

In the same period, the telecommunications industry was no slouch, either, in seeking strategic combinations, either on its own level or in combination with a publishing-entertainment giant; for example, the Viacom merger with Paramount

Communications. Is this a conglomerate? Not really because the differing layers of activity are much closer than in a traditional conglomerate, and there are simpler lines of potential synergism.

The Viacom-Paramount merger didn't come unstuck as did four other big ones. These were the AT&T-McCaw Electronics merger; the Bell Atlantic and Tele-Communications deal; the CBS-QVC marriage and the Southwestern Bell-Cox Enterprises joint venture. All were jockeying to plant their stake on the so-called "information superhighway," eager to cash in on the much anticipated multimedia breakout in which the consumer would just about be an electronic traveler, component, user or conduit.

It isn't difficult to say why so many big telephone, cable and television companies wanted in. The "superhighway," based on an endless network of home computers and telephones across the country, would provide a single device which would be able, as John Malone of Tele-Communications put it, "to control all the communications needs of a household." This could run the gamut from phoning mother to ordering a pizza to buying jackets and jeans to obtaining the news. Was the Bell Atlantic-TCI deal worth the sky-high $33 billion tab? Some doubted it, including, as it turned out, the two companies themselves.

Was there any common reason why all these multi-billion dollar deals collapsed? Weren't they, after all, examples of unadulterated, American entrepreneurism at work? Why couldn't they be? Let's examine them.

- *Bell Atlantic* - Tele-Communications: So much was stacked against this massive transaction. Senator Howard M. Metzenbaum, the Ohio Democrat, called the deal "a megamonster that will be costly to consumers" by making them pay higher phone and cable rates. The chutzpah of the nation's biggest of the Baby Bells seeking to marry the largest cable television company drew fears among Washington regulators and activists that two monopolies were being allowed to unite into a yet bigger monopoly that would allow them to clobber competition while also enjoying a competitive respite from each other. On a more direct level, the pending merger may have been killed by a cut in cable rates by the Federal Communications Commission that would have shrunk TCI's annual cash flow by about $175 million. Then there was the issue of contrasting cultures in each company— the staid, low-key demeanor of the telephone industry as epitomized by Raymond W. Smith, Bell Atlantic's chairman, and the bustling, hard-sell approach of the cable industry as per John C. Malone, TCI's president and CEO.

However, the most undigestible part of the transaction may have been its immense risk. Would TCI really spin off its cable properties within the Bell Atlantic region of Pennsylvania through Virginia, as the government demanded, that would drop 15 percent of all TCI subscribers? On an industry level, speculation ranged wildly on the potential for multimedia activity over the next five to 10 years: would it grow $5 billion, $10 billion, $50 billion a year? Not only was this ridiculous spread a source of extreme concern as to how much investment was warranted but what hardware should be pursued? Should it be video on demand or video telephones and how will consumers respond to all the new cables, general or specialized in nature? And, maybe the most needling question of all, would anyone have time for it all?

All these doubts were collected and reflected in a precipitous 20 percent drop in the stock of both Bell Atlantic and Tele-Communications since they had announced their merger in October 1993.

Inevitably, this melange of conflict and confusion proved just too much for the conservative Bell Atlantic. It announced that it was giving up its bid to buy Tele-Communications. Thus the largest planned merger of businesses in U.S. history was abandoned, a victim of too much size and too many imponderables. But, many asked, what would happen to other major pending deals in the multimedia field? Here's what happened.

- *AT&T* - McCaw Cellular Communications: This merger really seemed like one made in electronic heaven, because it paired the biggest telephone company (however cut down by government fiat) with the largest cellular-phone maker and operator. If it was true that Americans were becoming more mobile yet more conscious of family values, what made more sense than a telephone link between home and automobile, between people anywhere, those stationary and those on the move? Ah, but things are not what they seem, especially in a merger transaction worth $12.6 billion, that would create instant and constant communication.

First, it appeared to be a clearly synergistic combination of the major, long-distance network with the biggest cellular phone company, a far-near communications capability meeting a rapidly growing demand. Second, while everyone else was hopping on the information bandwagon and scanning the horizon to see what fantastic networks others were creating, AT&T and McCaw already had a simpler one in place, ready to go.

But no one figured on the legal bludgeon that could be wielded by a cherubic, smiling but tough jurist. On April 5, 1994, U.S. District Judge Harold H. Greene blocked the AT&T-McCaw merger because it would violate the antitrust ruling that had divided the old AT&T network into strictly regional networks. Judge Greene didn't kill the pending merger but delayed it until the participants could present an effective rebuttal and convince him to rescind his ruling.

Judge Greene must have been AT&T's nemesis. He was the jurist who oversaw the Bell system's breakup in 1984 and continued to enforce the antitrust agreement. Now he declared that the merger would reincarnate the old monolith since some of McCaw's cellular networks were owned or partly owned by the regional Bell companies.

Thus, AT&T would have to reformulate the deal by shedding several cellular phone systems in Los Angeles and Houston, both prime markets, and possibly elsewhere. If this were to be particularly punitive on the merged company's potential profits, it could conceivably kill the deal. But in August, the judge approved a waiver that AT&T submitted to prove that the merger would not violate the antitrust statutes and the merger was allowed to proceed.

Oddly, it was an AT&T "baby bell" that had blown the whistle. BellSouth Corporation, which owned a big chunk of the California and Texas cellular system, had complained of the antitrust implications. So, in one of those cruel or fortuitous ironies, whichever you prefer, a former AT&T unit had thrown a monkey wrench into the pending merger of its former parent.

- *Southwestern Bell* - Cox Enterprises: Four months after they announced their merger, these two sizeable companies decided to call off their $4.9 billion transaction. Under its provisions, Cox would have contributed 21 cable systems worth about $3.3 billion and Southwestern Bell was to have invested $1.6 billion.

  The reasons for the termination were simple. Southwestern said that it feared that a recent Federal Communications Commission's cable rate rise would curb its business potential and pare its profits. The two companies had hoped that their consolidation would increase Cox's 1.6 million cable subscribers to 4 million as well as offer additional services. But it was not merely the FCC's heavy hand that would hamper cash flows for cable companies that discouraged the two partners; it was the agency's potential to dream up yet tougher strictures.

  In calling off the merger. Southwestern Bell said it was interested in businesses that were less regulated. For his part, James Robbins, the president of the Cox Cable division of Cox Enterprises, said, colorfully, "The FCC dropped a bomb on the bridges to the interactive superhighway."

Buying Brands to Create a Bigger Market Basket

The RJR Nabisco megadeal was at its heart a strategic move to add well-known food brands to another strong collection, while reducing the dependence on the core tobacco business. But otherwise, in the late 1980s and early 1990s in the consumer goods manufacturing business, the principal guiding mergers involved the generalized acquiring the specific.

This tended to confirm, at least for the time being, the marketing impact of name-brand products over the always threatening but never decisive competition from private brands, store label or generic goods. In an uncertain economy, the name-brands simply had more staying power, more credibility. Supermarket shoppers tended to waffle over private labels or generics on the shelves. Take a chance on the so-so names, pocket the difference in price, or what? The well-perceived brands often won out in those countless quandaries.

Thus, in May 1994, when the German-Swiss pharmaceuticals giant, Sandoz Ltd., plunked down $3.7 billion for the Gerber Products Company, it was buying some of America's best-known baby product labels in food, clothes, toys and related goods. In baby food, the Midwest-based Gerber commanded 70 percent of the domestic baby-food product, so entrenched was its national brand. Almost immediately, Sandoz said it would introduce Gerber products into other markets, such as Europe, despite the fact that H. J. Heinz, another leading U.S. food producer, already held a big lead there. Sandoz's chief executive, Rolf W. Schweitzer, in announcing the deal, said that the Gerber purchase had been "on our shopping list for years because of its perfect fit" with Sandoz's nutrition business. Gerber would double that volume, he said, as well as add an important American base to Sandoz's essentially European business in nutrition products.

But, asked some of the tougher Wall Street analysts, wasn't Sandoz putting its money on a loser, considering Gerber's static sales in the U.S., its puny European presence, a limited potential for baby products internationally? Not to mention a purchase price of some 20 times Gerber's pretax income in 1993? It seemed to confirm a growing feeling among M&A mavens that foreigners in general were overpaying for their American acquisitions. But never mind, Sandoz appeared to be saying, "Nutrition is our second pillar," Schweitzer insisted.

In a proposed transaction, a second, well-known food producer, the Del Monte Foods Company, was to be acquired for $277 million in cash by an investor group led by Carlos Cabal Peniche, a Mexican businessman. For Del Monte, the sale was a fortunate and timely one. Since being sold by RJR Nabisco in a 1990 leveraged buyout, Del Monte had been forced to shed some of its best assets, such as Hawaiian Punch fruit drink and its European canned food operations. The LBO group which had paid $1.5 billion to acquire it from RJR Nabisco was now glad to sell it even if the selling price was much smaller than they had paid to buy it. But Grupo Cabal, as the foreign investor group was known, also agreed to pick up an undisclosed amount of Del Monte debt.

Strategically, Grupo Cabal wanted Del Monte in order to expand the group's market share in food in Latin America. Two years before, Senor Peniche had headed a group which paid $500 million to buy Del Monte Fresh Produce from Polly Peck International which had bought it from RJR prior to the LBO of the rest of Del Monte. The latter company operated plants and other facilities in Mexico, Central America and the Philippines. Obviously, a food giant was in the making in Latin America.

What was particularly interesting (at least to this writer who remembers the ubiquitous presence of Del Monte cans in his parents' cupboard) is that Del Monte, once a dominant player in the canned fruit-vegetable-snack food market, had fallen on lean times as result of the heavy debt accrued in its LBO deal and now was being recycled by a Latin-American investor syndicate. The Grupo Cabal-Del Monte deal aborted when Senior Peniche ran into some financial problems in Mexico. But the deal almost took place, raising a greater question. Was this the way that the U.S. industry was trending, being acquired by foreigners—first Gerber, then Del Monte, later the Neutrogena Company (soaps and fragrances), then the Regina Company (vacuum cleaners) for just some of the recent ones?

But there were many domestic mergers in consumer goods, too, involving both large and small firms. The Blockbuster Entertainment Corporation agreed after months of uncertainty to be bought by Viacom Inc., after the latter's merger with Paramount. Health-O-Matic Products, a weight-scale maker, paid $135 million for Mr. Coffee Inc., the coffee-maker company. And Rubbermaid Inc., the highly successful maker of non-electric housewares, decided to augment its brush line by taking over Empire Brushes, producer of brushes, brooms and mops.

And so it went. Companies buying others for their brands, for their production or to provide presence in the American or other markets, or for just plain strategy's sake.

Retailing and Wholesaling—Call It 'Store Wars'

In retailing and wholesaling, big companies merged and acquired so that they could be the kingpins in their own industry niches. So after weeks and weeks of saying no or maybe or never, R.H. Macy & Company succumbed to a merger offer from its biggest rival, Federated Department Stores, creating the nation's largest chain of department stores with sales of $13 billion. And in a marriage of the first- and third-biggest of the American food wholesalers, the Fleming Companies agreed in June 1994 to buy Scrivner Inc. to constitute the country's largest food distributor with sales of $19 billion.

Daring in its scope, the Federated-Macy merger at first drew skeptical predictions that it would ever come about. The skeptics cited the great size of the deal, a total of 365 department stores and belief that the government would surely step in to stay the merger of two such direct competitors. I also had the lingering suspicion that it was all a sort of feisty ploy by Federated's chairman, Allen I. Questrom, since back in 1988 Macy had been invited by a prior Federated management to rescue the company from the unwelcome arms of Canadian builder, Robert Campeau. Now Federated, minus Campeau but with Questrom, was turning the tables. So was Questrom serious? Yes, he was.

But some of my doubt and those of other skeptics began to disappear when Federated made a formal purchase offer after initially buying a 15 percent equity in Macy from the Equitable Life Insurance Company which had provided some of the funds for Macy's LBO in 1986. And even more doubt was dispelled when Questrom asked a bankruptcy judge (Macy then being in voluntary bankruptcy) to allow it to present its own reorganization to help Macy regain solvency.

However, the war wasn't yet over even though the Macy board, led by Laurence Tisch, began to waver in its support for Myron Ullman, Macy's chairman and CEO. On August 8, 1994, the New York Times emerged with an editorial, opposing the Federated-Macy merger on the grounds that it "raised serious antitrust questions." Federated already operated Bloomingdale's, Abraham & Straus and the Stern's department stores, three of the largest retailers in the metropolitan New York area and on the Atlantic Seaboard. Macy's had about 15 stores in the same general area. With Macy's under the Federated wing, "there would be even less pressure for the former rivals to cut prices to consumers. Local manufacturers of everything from pajamas to knickknacks would face fewer independent retailers bidding for their wares. And real estate developers would have fewer independent bids for space in their shopping malls." This editorial was patently a courageous statement for *The New York Times* since both Federated and Macy's were very important advertisers. But perhaps it wasn't all that altruistic. Perhaps someone in the *Times'* business department recalled that when Campeau swept up both Allied Stores and Federated, he began to pressure the media to give him special bulk discount advertising rates.

A week later, the Federal Trade Commission approved the merger. But a week after that, G. Oliver Koppell, the New York State Attorney General, announced that he would oppose the merger unless Federated would sell all 12 Macy's stores in the New York area, including the immense Herald Square store in Manhattan. But most observers assumed that the big retail merger would eventually be consummated after a compromise was reached with Koppell under which some but not all 12 stores would be sold. The disposition of six stores in the New York area was not a big price to pay for the biggest of all retailing mergers.

And then there was the odd spinoff situation at Kmart Corporation, the second-largest retailer after Wal-Mart Stores, Inc. Eager to cash in on the individual market value of four of Kmart's specialty-store subsidiaries, Joseph Antonini, the parent company's scrappy but beleaguered chief executive, and his board proposed in 1994 to sell 20 to 30 percent stakes to the public in Builders Square, the Sports Authority, Office Max and the Borders-Waldenbooks chains. Antonini, pressed by some protracted negative results in his company, contended that the true value of those retail entities was not being reflected in Kmart's market price. This was due, he said, to the poor performance of the company's core discount-store division.

But by allowing the public to buy pieces of those businesses through a public stock issue, he asserted, the chain's real value would be determined and the proceeds could be applied by the company to repairing and remodelling the core discount stores. Even before the stockholders' meeting, several major holders of Kmart stock said that they would not vote their shares in favor of the proposal. Reasons given were that since the corporation's major profits were emanating from those specialty chains, the spinoffs would not help the core stores but would simply establish a market value for themselves. In other words, it was a management ploy to obtain an investment in Kmart without taking any pains to correct the real problem.

Sure enough, the proposal was roundly defeated at the meeting, confounding both Antonini and his board members. A few weeks later, they temporarily solved the problem by passing a resolution that the specialty chains would be sold in toto, or 100 percent rather than merely small stakes, with the proceeds being used at the discount stores simultaneously with new efforts being undertaken to right its course.

There will surely be more to come. Kmart, in an effort to pare down to what counts, had sold a portion of its Pace membership warehouse club chain to Wal-Mart's Sam's Wholesale Clubs. Hence, it can be assumed that other Kmart properties are also for sale, quite possibly the entire company, although with sales of $37 billion in 1993 it would make quite a mouthful for someone to chew. BUT—remember. Size is no longer any barrier to a merger, as we pointed out earlier.

Meanwhile, a big deal worth some $600 million was racked up in April 1994 by Revco D.S., Inc. and Hook-Superx Inc., two large drug-store groups, seeking to create the nation's second-largest such retail chain after the Walgreen Company. When completed, the deal would expand Revco to almost 2,400 stores in the midwest, southeast, and northeast with total revenues of about $4.54 billion. Behind it all, of course, was the pending, national health-care statute, prompting already substantial drug chains to swallow up one another to gain more market share.

Forming Big Complexes in Publishing and Media

Plenty of action was also underway in publishing and media. The deal deluxe, already mentioned, is the Viacom merger with Paramount Communications. But shortly before that, Paramount itself had acquired Macmillan Inc., the 150-year old book publisher. With that $553 million, cash transaction, Paramount enhanced its status as the biggest American book publisher. Paramount would command sales of almost $2 billion when the merger was consummated.

Germany's Bertlesmann A.G. kept busy, too. In June, it purchased for a reported $350 million the women's magazine division of The New York Times Company, including Family Circle, with 5.1 million in paid circulation, and McCall's, with 4.6 million in circulation. Also included were such other magazines as Child, Fitness, and American Homestyle, as well as a unit that creates new magazines and one-time publications, a women's sports and event-marketing business and a telemarketing subsidiary. Bertlesmann bought the magazine group through its Gruner—Jahr USA Publishing, its American publishing arm, a move that propelled G+J into a major player in U.S. magazine publishing. Besides its Parents and YM magazines, G+J liked the family-and-fitness niche and its parent let it flex its muscle.

Newspapers also were buying and selling. In 1993, the Times startled the newspaper world by buying the Boston Globe for about $1.1 billion in cash and stock. Newspaper insiders claimed that the Globe, finally emerging from the clammy New England recession, was in play, partly because the owning family wanted to assure continuity for the paper and security for itself. The Times said that it wanted the Globe because it was one of America's great newspapers; it would provide technological synergy with the Times; that the New England economic turndown was over and that ownership of the Globe's facilities would give the Times a New England base in which to print its newspapers.

For those who wondered why the Times wanted another large metropolitan newspaper when it was still weathering the recession that affected almost all big cities, the answer seemed to be that the big New York newspaper company had been pleased with the small-town papers it had accumulated and was convinced that it could have a similar, pleasant experience with the Globe.

In July 1994, a month after the Globe merger was announced, the Times sold its three British golf magazines to IPC Magazines, a subsidiary of the British-Dutch publisher, Reed Elsevier P.C. This transaction was not related to the Globe deal and represented only an arrangement which had been in the making several years and happened to mature close in the wake of the newspaper merger, a Times spokesman said.

In Chicago, the Chicago Sun-Times, a tabloid engaged in a lively competition with the more substantial and financially secure Chicago Tribune, was bought for $180 million by a company controlled by Conrad Black. A Canadian, Black had been building an international newspaper network. In the U.S., the American Publishing Company, a subsidiary of Black's Hollinger Inc., already owned 97 daily newspapers and 71 weeklies mostly in small midwestern cities and towns. Based in Vancouver, British Columbia, Hollinger also owned or maintained large interests in newspapers in Canada, Britain, Israel and Australia.

The Chicago Sun-Times, which had been owned since 1986 by Adler & Shaykin, a New York investment firm specializing in leveraged buyouts, would be by far the largest property in American Publishing Company. The newspaper's average weekly circulation was 535,793 against the Trib's 690,842 copies. The agreement also included the sale of 60 weekly and biweekly newspapers published by the Sun-Times.

What was motivating all this? All the shifting and flux reflected strategic moves by the domestic and foreign media to obtain better market share or market entry, to clean their books of either lower-profit products or those not in their mainstream and get set for the bright domestic economy that was certain to come.

Hostile Bids Roil the Banks and Insurance Firms

Banks and insurance companies were two of the most active— and bloodiest—merger arenas in the late 1980s and the early

1990s, intensified by several hostile offers which grew very heated as they approached their denouements. In one or two cases, the ultimate conclusion was not clear as announced and waiting bidders implied that they were biding their time before making their final acquisition offers.

In a $3.2 billion deal, Conseco Inc., an investment company in the insurance and financial-services field, bested the General Electric Company in capturing the Kemper Corporation with a higher offer of $67 a share over the rival's $60 a share cash offer. Conseco's offer was for $56 a share in cash and $11 in Conseco common stock. The victory was a severe disappointment for GE, whose offer a month earlier had at first stunned the Kemper board and then compelled the directors to put the company up for sale. Conseco then jumped in and emerged triumphant after several steps in the bidding process. Without outwardly licking its wounds, GE immediately withdrew when Conseco made its final, higher bid, in June 1994.

Kemper was a lush target. A quiet, steady company, it operated two life-insurance companies, owned a number of real-estate holdings, had the seventh-largest mutual fund and an investment advisory business. Conseco said it would sell the Kemper life-insurance companies and real estate for $1.35 billion to Conseco Capital Partners, an investment fund Conseco had organized early in 1994. Conseco would keep the rest of the Kemper properties and retain the Kemper name for them.

For Conseco, the acquisition strategy was clear. Because Kemper wasn't followed by many Wall Street analysts, its stock price had remained less than those of other insurance companies so that the purchase price could be kept relatively moderate. This would help Conseco to digest the acquisition, which, in turn, would allow its own insurance companies to benefit from the deal by now being able to offer variable annuities to supplement the fixed-rate annuities Conseco had been selling. The addition of Kemper's insurance business would, in other words, give Conseco's investment company the flexibility it needed to diversify its investment business.

It was not the first of Conseco Capital Partners' recent acquisitions. In May, it had put up $350 million to buy the Statesman Group, an insurance company and seller of annuities. The Kemper and Statesman purchases capped a binge of insurance acquisitions that Conseco had been making since 1982; those 11 acquisitions were obviously intended not merely to increase the market presence of the Carmel, California-based Conseco but hopefully also to imbue it with the efficiencies promised by economy of scale. But in November 1994, before the consummation of the deal with Kemper, Conseco became so concerned by a precipitous drop in its stock that it withdrew its offer.

If Conseco was a hot pursuer in the insurance field, the PNC Bank Corporation, based in Pittsburgh, was no tortoise, either.

In May and June of 1994 alone, PNC completed three acquisitions increasing its exposure in the asset management business, expanding its number of branches and boosting its market share in mortgage banking. The aggressive Pennsylvania bank plunked down a total of $687 million mostly in cash for those three transactions. In the largest one, in May PNC agreed to buy the 51-branch First Eastern Corporation in Wilkes-Barre, Pa., for about $330 million, thus assuming the biggest market share in banking in northeastern Pennsylvania. Then in June, PNC signed a letter of intent to buy the mortgage-servicing portfolio of the Associates Corporation of North America, a division of the Ford Motor Company. With this acquisition of the $10-billion mortgage portfolio for $117 million in cash, PNC pushed itself into the top 10 mortgage servicers with its portfolio of $46 billion.

Later in June, PNC paid $240 million in cash and notes for BlackRock Financial Management L.P., thus also becoming one of the biggest fixed-income management companies.

The asset management business also witnessed a buying frenzy as one bank after another moved in on the struggling mutual fund industry, dangling bait which was eagerly snapped up. The Mellon Bank Corporation, for example, acquired the Dreyfus Corporation and First Union Corporation bought Lieber & Company. More such deals were expected as mutual funds found their competition growing from banks and as their costs rose and assets fell in value due to slumping markets.

The scramble was almost as furious in banking as bigger institutions swooped down on smaller ones. Shawmut National Corporation, the growing, Boston-based bank, made seven acquisitions also in May and June. Among them were first the 10 branches of the Northeast Federal Corporation and then that entire bank with branches in Massachusetts, Connecticut and New York. Shawmut only days before, had completed a purchase of the New Dartmouth Bank in Manchester, New Hampshire, People's Bankcorp in Worcester, Mass. and was awaiting regulatory approval to complete its purchase of Gateway Financial Corporation, Norwalk, Connecticut and two other banks.

Unlike in Pittsburgh and Boston, where the larger banks were swallowing smaller ones, the New York banking market was relatively static in this respect. In 1991, the Chemical Bank merged with Manufacturers Hanover Corporation in the last big bank merger and Chemical then steadily pursued a policy of closing more than 130 branches. The reason for the subsequent acquisition hiatus was generally assumed to be that the larger banks were concentrating instead on recovering from their binge of bad loans. In addition, banking sources claimed that these institutions were also more eager to court the better-heeled customers who favor banking by cash machines, telephone and home/office computers than in frequenting the branch banks.

In November 1993, however, the calm ended. The Republic New York Corporation of Manhattan made a hostile bid for the Green Point Savings Bank of Flushing, New York, targeting Green's giant retained earnings of $758 million. The 125-year old Green Point then was already in the process of converting to a shareholder-owned corporation through a $600 million to $800 million public stock issue. It was a bonanza in the making for all the insiders. They would get 30 percent of the company and all the top management and trustees would automatically become millionaires, if they weren't already that.

Now Republic, a highly-regarded if somewhat swaggering institution, gave that plan a sharp kick. It proposed to pay nothing for the bank directly but offered a $100 million special-interest payment to depositors, similar to the manner through which it had earlier acquired two smaller banks, the Manhattan Savings Bank and the Williamsburgh Savings Bank.

Not that the Green Point scenario of rewarding its top brass was anything like unique. The compensation program was similar to those conversion plans effected by mutual savings banks, except that the Green Point plan was the largest in terms of dollars. And the bank's management and trustees fought back briskly to protect it in a dogfight that lasted for weeks. It ended with Green Point successfully defending itself.

The Republic-Green Point imbroglio seemed to unloose the conservatism that had been dogging the New York banks. A number of smaller banks then got busy scooping up even smaller ones in the New York-Long Island area, until one of major proportions erupted in the savings bank field. Dime Bankcorp, parent of the Dime Savings Bank of New York, made a merger offer for the Anchor Savings Bank. The offer was readily accepted by Anchor in July 1994. The combination of Dime's 34 branches and Anchor's 65 would create the largest, publicly traded thrift institution outside of California. The partners' strategy: fill in and augment the banks' coverage in the city and Long Island.

Banks, M&A experts have stated, will be among the most active merger participants in the rest of the 1990s. That's not hard to believe since many around the country are only now in clean shape, having rid themselves of bad loans and investments and are flush with the scent of a more confident consumer.

It's a Brand New Sky in Airlines and Aircraft

Much has changed in the airline and aircraft industries. Since Federal deregulation, the airlines have been harder hit than almost any other industry in recent years. Gone are Eastern and PanAm and a bunch of smaller airlines. Delta and US Air have shot up in prominence while newer, minor airlines have surfaced such as UltrAir, Tower Air and others. It's a brand new sky these days.

But in the 1990s, the aircraft industry took the spotlight.

Few merger transactions had the drama and suspense of the Grumman-Martin Marietta-Northrop fracas which lasted a month in the spring of 1994. It left Martin Marietta

Corporation bitter and bleeding. Grumman, the old and bat-
tered Long Island, New York, military contractor-aircraft maker,
which was the target company, was left stunned and wondering if $2.1 billion were really enough salve for the loss of its
independence.

Grumman's future had dimmed when the Pentagon began
its long string of cutbacks in military hardware and aircraft,
some 65 percent from its 1985 budget level. Martin Marietta,
which had been acquiring some smaller military contractors,
began to eye Grumman for its huge size and reported availability. In March, Martin Marietta offered to buy Grumman for $1.9
billion or $55 a share. But across the country from Grumman's
Long Island base, the Northrop Corporation suddenly felt the
uncomfortable winds of change fanning across it as the management looked at the pending Martin Marietta-Grumman
deal. Just a few days later, Northrop placed a higher, unsolicit-
ed bid for $2.04 billion, or $60 a share. Northrop hadn't been
making acquisitions, unlike rival Martin Marietta, and decided
it needed more critical mass to survive in a smaller, more
parched industry.

On April 4, Northrop won Grumman for a slightly higher
bid of $62 a share. The merger wheel kept turning, with
Lockheed Corporation, another major aircraft producer and
military contractor, waking up one morning to find itself a hot
takeover target. Was it true, as someone told this writer, that
"the M&A game heats up most when the economy is bad or an
industry is in trouble..."? Or is it just that every industry must
respond to competitive drives and market changes?

Were Lockheed and Martin Marietta preparing to merge
and create a $22 billion military hardware colossus? That was
the credible rumor several months after Grumman was lured
away by Northrop in Los Angeles, a deal that, while big at the
time, was much less than a Lockheed-Martin Marietta merger
would create. It didn't take very long for those rumors to materialize (the next day in fact) when both companies announced
their superdeal.

If hurt feelings lingered from the swift, unexpected resolution of the Grumman takeover, it was much worse and more
layered in the case of UAL Corporation, the corporate parent of

United Airlines. In mid-1994, the UAL shareholders awarded various employee groups 55 percent of the company's stock for a $4.9 billion package of concessions. This put United Airlines in the unique position of being the country's biggest employee-owned company. It was a triumph indeed for the workers who had sacrificed wages and other necessities in the hope that it would pay off.

However, even the victory after almost a decade faced a welter of uncertainty. Employee groups fought one another through those years and were still fighting. There had been threats of a takeover by several of America's more merger-prone businessmen who could still come after the airline. There had been a 29-day pilots' strike, a symbol of unrest that might arise again. All this with a background also of previous employee buyout efforts, cutbacks and unhappy rumors.

But the unions involved were not anxious to take over in a docile manner. They asked that three of UAL's top executives be let go, including Stephen Wolf, who had been CEO for seven years. Gerald Greenwald, former vice chairman of Chrysler Corporation, was the union's selection to replace Wolf. Among the genial Greenwald's headaches would be smoothing over the bad relations of the employees who had voted in favor of owning United Airlines and the many who hadn't. The situation was also clouded by union corruption and by varying demands on salary by different groups among the 28,000 employee-owners.

Would employee owners be tougher than public or private managements? Greenwald was about to find out.

How Strategic is the Strategic Merger?

Perhaps the only question that remains is whether the merger or acquisition is actually made for strategy's sake or really is a copout by a lazy management.

The latter charges were leveled against American Home Products in buying American Cyanamid, that it was little more than a lateral expansion of more brands with little vision as to the future. But American Home Products felt otherwise.

Similarly, the same sort of confusion and questioning sur-
rounded ITT Corporation's acquisition of the Madison Square
Garden Corporation in conjunction with Cablevision Systems
Inc. in August 1994. Why was an insurance-hotel-financial services conglomerate getting into sports entertainment? Was it
an ego trip by CEO Rand Araskog? Not a bit, he said, adding
that the acquisition fit with ITT's Sheraton Hotels. And why
was Federated Department Stores buying Macy's—to swallow
and regurgitate a competitor in curtailed, altered form and thus
squash the competition? Or to truly seek added market share
and outstrip May Department Stores as the leading U.S. depart-
ment-store operator?

The answer to the validity of the strategic merger is, of
course, that each must be looked at individually, now and later,
to determine the real worth of the transaction. Not just in dollar return but in benefits to the companies, the shareholders
and the employees.

chapter 4

To Buy or Die: Examining M&A Philosophy

Is it really buy or die? In the last two-and-a-half decades, we have gone from conglomerates to leveraged buyouts to dissolutions of conglomerates to strategic mergers. Now in the 1990s merger boom, the second biggest in American history, business consolidations have become so intertwined into U.S. business that few executives, academics, government officials, financial executives and professional observers question their worth or contribution to economic progress.

Who knows how American business will evolve? Joseph H. Flom knows.

The M&A World According to Flom

For 45 years Joseph H. Flom, the senior partner of the major New York law firm of Skadden, Arps, Slate, Meagher & Flom, has been perhaps the nation's most prominent attorney in the mergers and acquisitions field. "My philosophy is that trends in all types of businesses, and in all things in society, start deliberately, increase in volume, then go to extremes," Flom says. "This results in a correction, in new regulation. And then the trends start moving the other way."

"Merger movements run about 10 years or so," said Flom during an interview in his Manhattan office. "As in the previous merger waves, the current one involves business-oriented transactions and is for the most part economically justified. People get very euphoric about it but you start seeing abuses as we did from 1973 to 1989 and that is the case today. Yet many of these mergers are legitimate business combinations."

When viewed as a group, Flom said, "Mergers are being driven by liquidity, money availability or what I call 'high-octane' paper. Right now, we are in the early stages of a merger boom but, like the others, I think it will eventually lead to new legislation."

He thinks that the current merger wave will continue in industries in which previous merger waves created large combinations. "It's very active now in the telecommunications areas and related fields. Banks will continue to be active in mergers. Public utilities will become more involved. And insurance and drug companies," Flom says.

As a business writer first for the *New York Herald Tribune* and then for the *New York Times*. I became aware early on of the stern, august role Joe Flom was playing in the field of business consolidations. He became a sort of gray eminence advising chief executive officers which way to turn, what offensive or defensive moves to take, whom to believe and not and what media people to let through the door. After receiving his law degree at Harvard in 1948 and being admitted to the New York bar in 1949, he began his career as the first associate of a three-lawyer firm (Skadden Arps Slate) when the traditional, button-down law firms wouldn't hire him because he was Jewish. Then he became a pioneer in the leveraged buyout movement of the 1980s as legal counsel to Kohlberg Kravis & Roberts and to R. H. Macy & Company and was involved in a plethora of legal and charitable activities. His reputation grew as a "lawyer's lawyer." Many awards, honors, and accolades came to him. At 70, he's still formidable and a bit forbidding.

As Flom sees it, the following conditions prevail today in the field of mergers and acquisitions:

There is an improved flow of capital, trade accessibility and international communications. Funds of various types are becoming more available for acquisitions. Large, established funds both nationally and internationally are willing to invest in deals. Large leveraged buyout funds are significantly under-invested but an estimated $30 billion has already been raised. Several of these have become restructuring funds aimed at purchasing troubled companies. Banks are expected to return to acquisition lending and bank mergers have served to strengthen bank portfolios. New forms of lending vehicles are being developed. The junk bond market is stabilizing although it probably will not be used as a credit source for hostile acquisitions. Cross-border and strategic transactions will continue to fuel activity. With foreign acquirers still benefiting from cheap dollars, European and Japanese players have become increasingly sophisticated as deal makers.

In foreign markets, Europe is expected to continue to expand. "The European market has been mainly strategy-driven and it harbors corporations that are seeking to expand their international presence with the unification of the Common Market," Flom says. In 1991, a study by a major accounting firm found that the European Common Market had replaced North America as the hottest region for investment, attracting $24 billion. "This, compounded with the opening of Eastern Europe and the Soviet Union, will offer broad opportunities for expansion but may drain potential funds for U.S. transactions," Flom says.

He sees a potentially expanding Asian market because many nations, such as South Korea, Hong Kong, Singapore, Thailand and Malaysia, have amassed huge cash surpluses. They are expected to react to the pressure of global competition by restructuring their economies and by looking outside their home markets in search for acquisitions and joint ventures.

"Competition and rationalization are the strategic considerations driving acquisition activity," says Flom. "More companies have begun to expand and explore joint licensing and research and development agreements as a first step to or in place of direct mergers. Partial acquisitions or strategic investments are also becoming more common. There is a decrease in the number of hostile acquisitions, although there is an increase in the number of corporate governance proposals."

Industries which did not fully participate in the last great merger wave because of regulatory restrictions, such as the banking, insurance and utilities fields, will now join the merger parade. Flom also noted a return to negotiated, strategic transactions in contrast to the "large auctions" of the recent past and an increase in the number of transactions involving a substantial stock component.

"There seems to be evidence that the availability of cash and other acceptable securities is the major factor in accelerating or dampening takeover activity," he says. "There is also evidence indicating that during takeover booms markets tend to be buoyant. Successive merger waves proceeded apace although the legislative restrictions ending the previous wave were still in effect. And while public policy changes may act as a provoking cause of significant decline in the market and takeover activity, they do not stop activity totally."

He adds, "In my view, no adequate methodology for evaluating who is right has been developed; nor is there any meaningful consensus on which effects should be evaluated, or how such effects should be weighed, nor which type of transactions should be aggregated. Even when attempts to isolate and evaluate specific elements have been made, there is a multiplicity of factors raising questions as to how meaningful the conclusions are."

During the mid-to-late 1980s, he said, "Despite complaints from dislocated workers, and in the face of the greatest merger wave in our history, the economy as a whole was creating jobs at an unprecedented rate. Moreover, to the extent that mergers guaranteed or restructuring caused job loss, one must ask whether that was good or bad in that the failure to address excess labor and inefficiencies might well lead to greater losses ultimately to foreign competition." He added, with a rueful smile, "We go out the same door we came in. One can argue about the social impact of mergers. But they will thrive as long as there are economic dislocations or anomalies which they can effectively address and I believe that those anomalies will continue to be created providing for additional activity."

But what is it that gets under the hide of corporate senior management which pushes it into a "buy or die" syndrome?

"There are three factors which encourage merger consideration," he replied. "One, the uncertainty on the part of chief executives on the permanency of their tenure. You see that all around. Two, international competitive pressures. And three, the realization of chief executives that there is a market for their skills."

That brings us to the example of Glaxo.

Issue: Going It Alone, or Buying Others to Grow

It may be a foreign company but Glaxo Holdings PLC, the British pharmaceuticals giant, is a good example to put under a microscope and see what happened when the 68-year old chairman, Paul Girolami, refused to go the merger-acquisition route. The Italian immigrant, a professional accountant, built Glaxo into a super-company during his 13-year reign as its chief executive officer and then chairman. One of his chief accomplishments was the development of new, important, best-selling drugs, Zantac in particular. This ulcer-fighting medication became the world's best selling in its field. Its growing market share only convinced Girolami that he was right to spurn distracting acquisitions in a field where buyouts were booming. But his luck ran out.

First, Glaxo's chief executive officer, Ernest Mario, who had succeeded Girolami as CEO, quit in March 1993 when Girolami and the board refused to allow him to go ahead with an acquisition of the Warner-Lambert Company. His way, insiders said, was greased by Girolami who insisted that a business's fate depended upon developing new products and promptly gave those who disagreed the boot.

Then competitors came out with their own products like Zantac and generics also sprouted, raising potentially adverse effects on Glaxo's top- and bottom-lines. This could happen even before the Zantac patents terminate in 1996. It was especially disturbing since Glaxo in 1994 had no new hot products to bring to the market.

Finally, as the Glaxo board saw Merck & Company, Smith Kline Beecham snapping up other companies to become more diversified and more powerful within the pharmaceuticals and medical fields, a movement began to replace Girolami. He agreed to leave a year before schedule and was succeeded by Richard B. Sykes, a research-and-development expert who had replaced Mario as CEO. Sykes promptly began exploring acquisition possibilities.

Was Girolami wrong to think that he could rely on a single product that brought in more than 40 percent of Glaxo sales and an even higher percentage of its profits? Obviously, that was wrong. But, that aside, the dearth of any blockbuster medications brewing in Glaxo's pipeline also indicates some problems in the R&D sector. One hot product should foster another, especially one as successful as Zantac. Whether the fault was Girolami's or Sykes' isn't as important as the fact that no business can thrive on just one product and that was the road that Glaxo had taken.

Mergers and acquisitions, especially strategically-based ones, make sense. But it also makes sense for companies able to develop world-class products to give considerable priority to developing others. Are the two strategies mutually exclusive? Of course not. But relying exclusively on one at the expense of the other is a dangerous practice. What counts is a blend of common sense and flexibility.

But, at the same time, a rush to acquire as a way of growing doesn't make much sense, either. It's no great feat nowadays to buy companies that seem to offer salvation for a desperate CEO, totally unlike the Paul Girolami's of the world. It wasn't before, either. As Joseph Flom said, comparing the present with the past, "We go out the same door we came in."

Things Don't Change, They Just Stay the Same

Here's what someone told me years ago that pertains to the M&A mentality of some major CEOs:

"The trouble is that they began to listen to their own public relations people, that the only direction is up, that you can go from one acquisition to another without stopping, not worrying about the equity that remains and letting the long-term debt pile up," he said. "You talk to a roomful of analysts and see their tongues hanging out, waiting for the big projection, and you give it to them. We are optimists by nature and if they invite us to 'optimize,' well, dammit, we 'optimize.'"

"Then what happens to us? We pile up long-term debt, we overproject our earnings, we build high hopes for our operating people and they let us down—and then it all shows up in the earnings. The analysts catch hell from the institutions... Then, of course, the government guys start nodding their heads, because here is evidence that they have been right all along. They really have no problem, those fellows. They just sit in their offices and figure out ways to kick us around. They aren't investors, bankers or operators of any kind. I'm not trying to knock them for the sake of knocking, but in some ways they're the least responsible of all... It's all our own fault. I don't say that I suffer from gluttony, but we let our public-relations guys take over or maybe we wanted them to..."

When do you think this merger maven, who was speaking of "them" and meant "me, too," said all that? Those candid, salty words came from one of the great, contemporary American merger-makers of twenty-five years ago, who allowed me to quote him anonymously in my earlier book, "Welcome to Our Conglomerate—You're Fired!" I will still keep my word not to identify him but there's such a relevance now a quarter-century plus afterward that you can see that the instinct to "buy, buy, buy" hasn't changed much.

Now, let's talk about how the businessman might behave after just having made a deal. Is there a smart way to behave?

Building the Strategic Merger

So it's a done deal... the lenders, banks, shareholders and media have gone home to gloat or sulk. The employees of both companies are holding their collective breaths. The media are satiated, ready to chase someone else's deal. And there you are, sitting on top of it all, wondering just what you did, why and how you can come out of it all with body and soul intact and, of course, a pile of dollars or paper. What, in other words, comes next?

"Accentuate the positive, 'decentuate' the negative but don't fool with Mr. In-Between," advises Peter J. Solomon, the investment banker and M&A maven, recalling the old ballad, "Accentuate the Positive."

"The goal in any strategic merger is to build strength on strength. In other words, take what's good and what you are good at and build on them," he adds. "What you don't do well, you get rid of. That's what makes the strategic merger not just a merger for merger's sake."

But hasn't that appraisal already been done in the "due diligence" phase of the merger-acquisition process wherein the target company's assets and books are examined? No, it really hasn't. The way it works, the management of the target company isn't compelled to show everything, just what it wants to. Also, it may well be inclined to hide a good deal in case the transaction doesn't go through and also may be subject to carelessness and inefficiency in monitoring all as is the buying company.

How many mergers and acquisitions fail? Between 30 and 40 percent, merger experts say. Now admittedly this range isn't exact because opinions differ on what constitutes success and what doesn't. But most M&A mavens I speak to freely admit that a large number of mergers or acquisitions do not produce the amount of mutual benefits—the return on capital or investment or the spectrum of benefits—that were portrayed in the rooms where the deals were cooked up.

But what hasn't changed very much are the main criteria of successful consolidations. They are earnings improvement, return on capital, better stock prices, market share of the buying and selling companies, production, remuneration of the top executives, rank-and-file income, product and service improvements and the effect on the local economies.

Now let's talk about how to achieve your strategic goals.

Back to you, the boss. Looking over the new company, its parts and assets, you assign a short team to support or not support retention or disposition, which you have probably already decided anyway. The strong, vibrant parts you will keep, the weak you will get rid of as fast as you can. But what's left is the "in-between," the relatively steady performers that should be retained because they are the most reliable revenue-and-profit makers. From here on for a bit, let's talk about actual cases and how the strategy-within-a-strategy worked.

In January 1988, Robert Campeau, the feisty, unpredictable Canadian builder and mall developer, announced an offer for Federated Department Stores. Already the owner of Allied Stores Corporation, which owned the Jordan Marsh stores in New England and Florida, the Bon Marche department stores in Seattle and others, Campeau now wanted Federated's Bloomingdale's, Abraham & Straus and Stern's in New York, Burdine's in Florida, Bullock's and I. Magnin in California and other leading stores. And he won Federated, too, after raising his bid several times, outwitting both Federated's management and a rival bid from R. H. Macy & Company.

What to do? The core department store groups in Federated had to be retained since, after all, that was why Campeau had gone for the company in the first place. But Campeau had an enormous pile of debt which he was confident he could handle, even though in an interview in Federated's Cincinnati offices he told me that he had three scenarios reflecting great, modest and poor economic conditions. Under all of them, he insisted, his Federated-Allied merger could thrive, and he meant it. "My researchers," he said, "assure me that it can be done."

His strategy, during the height of the hostile tender offer, encompassed first getting Macy's off his back, so he sold his Bullock's-I. Magnin stores to Macy's for $1.1 billion. This helped him reduce his debt by that amount while for Macy's the transaction ultimately plunged it into bankruptcy. To further lighten his debt load and obtain funds for remodeling his core stores and to pay for the severance bite covering employees to be discharged, he then sold the Foley department stores in Texas and the Filene's fashion-store chain to May Department Stores for another $1.2 billion.

Then, as if that weren't enough, Campeau staged several "internal mergers," consolidating regional store groups into several super-regional chains with one headquarters staff and location, eliminating hundreds of duplicate jobs. This took place in Florida where the long-operating Maas Brothers and Jordan Marsh stores were combined under Burdines; in Ohio where the Lazarus stores became the umbrella and name for Rike's in Dayton and Shillito's in Columbus; and in Boston where all the New England stores were moved under the Jordan Marsh banner. All this cutting and filling wrought much cost savings in terms of fewer people, rental costs and other economies.

The asset sales and internal consolidations brought forth peals of self-congratulations from the Campeau headquarters in Cincinnati. Each disposition of the store groups brought, as Peter Solomon recalls it, "simply huge prices. What was more, their new owners eventually did much better with them than Campeau had done. Still Bob Campeau looked very smart. Until something else became clear."

What he did was to ignore the core businesses, confusing their managements with outrageous demands, cutting their operating budgets, pressuring suppliers and major media to give him hefty pool discounts. Such strong divisions as Bloomingdale's, A&S, Burdine's and Lazarus found themselves hamstrung with less "open-to-buy" budgets and unhappy vendors and advertising media. Staff morale hit rock bottom. "He just screwed up the main business," summed up Solomon.

The moral: Campeau did the right thing by selling off nonessential businesses but he did the wrong thing by fooling around with "Mr. In-Between." The negative effect helped spin Federated into a two-year tussle with voluntary bankruptcy from which it finally emerged in 1993. These days, you can't get anyone at Federated to even mention Campeau's name.

Examining Several Merger Philosophies

In the process of writing this book, I asked a number of professionals if there was such a thing as a philosophy of mergers. After they verbally blinked a few times, three responded.

Peter J. Solomon's credo: never do a merger without checking your instincts. "Chief executive officers often understand things before they can articulate them," says Solomon. "They understand more than their boards do. The CEO really tries to lead his board toward understanding. But in doing so, he has laid on so much horse-manure that they don't understand him."

Conversely, the danger is that a CEO may himself be talked into a merger because of dollars-and-cents advantages rather than other important considerations, Solomon warns. "The point is that a CEO should not make a merger unless he instinctively understands it. Will it fulfill the company's needs or just cover them up or delay them? That's the real question any guy sitting on top of a pending merger or acquisition must ask himself."

Ralph Nelson points out that target shareholders gain; bidding shareholders lose. Nelson, professor of economics at Queens College of the City University of New York, has followed the American merger movement for more than four decades. In 1959, he wrote a seminal book, "Merger Movements in American History" (Princeton University Press), which dealt with the nation's first big merger wave from 1897 to 1902. "That wave basically created the big business movement," he said. "Before the turn of the century, American industry consisted of a large number of small- and medium-sized firms. But after the first wave, we had the beginnings of such big companies as United States Steel, International Harvester, American Tobacco and many others who came after them."

Professor Nelson has some cogent bits of observation and philosophy about the current merger wave.

"Much is asked about who gains or who loses in business mergers," he said. "I agree with Professor Michael Jensen of Harvard that the shareholders of the target company gain an average of 30 percent higher value for their stock. Who loses? The shareholders of the bidding company gain very little.

"But mergers often assume an aura of controversy," he added. "All the hue and cry comes from the press and from the bidders who complain about the pressure to raise their price. A lot of this is colorful and newsworthy. The 'poison pills' and the other defense tactics and the colorful names given to them make very good press. The considerable preoccupation with the maneuvering of the contenders has tended to cover the economic substance which is to improve management and make the business more responsive to change."

Mergers have been a continuing activity for many years, Professor Nelson said, "because business is always seeking to grow and change in order to survive. Businessmen will seek any means of doing it. Investing in new plant and equipment and growing that way is one way. Growing by merger is another way. But they are not mutually exclusive and business will continue to do both as an ongoing process."

Laurence S. Grafstein says that too many companies are risk averse. "I go back to Peter Drucker who says that business's biggest mistakes are missed opportunities," says Grafstein, head of the telecommunications practice at Wasserstein, Perella & Company, the New York investment bankers. "A number of companies are risk averse because they become increasingly less certain about opportunities that present themselves, and fail to make deals.

"It's sort of ironic," Grafstein says. "Everyone talks about the transactions that people do and are eager to say it took too much money; the CEO didn't do this or that, but very rarely do investors criticize companies for the opportunities they miss. Too often, managements are aware of opportunities that make sense but elect to ignore them to play it safe."

part two

Moving and Shaking

chapter 5

The Typical American Merger

The process of creating a merger could be as chaotic as one of those shtick in a Marx Brothers comedy. One guy peering through a telescope in some high-rise building sees another eye looking through a telescope directly at him. One blinks. The other blinks back. That ignites the merger game as it is played in the 1990s.

If the players could, they would stare through windows, brick and stone across town, trying to read the other's mind and ferret out if the same idea was popping there. Is it buying, or selling, or just dealing? In today's frantic, business merger scene, it's not impossible that every businessperson is thinking merger at the same time or on the same day.

It's real-life Monopoly, not played on a table but on a grand scale that can bridge cities, even continents and cultures. And it tends to spawn people, lots of people.

The fact is that there's a sort of raw mathematical beauty in the way mergers and acquisitions build. First, there's one executive who is involved who leads to another. That's two. They consult on the idea with others in their companies. That's six, at least. They call in their financial advisors. That's eight. These consult with banks, insurance companies, pension funds. That's somewhere about 48 to 60. As these study the matter, plug it into their PC's or laptops, and shoot directives off to underlings, the number of those involved grows to double, triple, quadruple. Before you know it, there's a small regiment tramping in those woods.

Ironically enough, all that began with one idle thought in one person's mind who sat in an office, stared at a computer, read the Wall Street Journal or eyed the company's operating statement irritably or avariciously. Buy, sell, or maybe just get an investment banker moving?

Guard Your Idea; It Could Be Contagious

Before we get to our profile of a typical merger in the great wave that seems never to abate in American business, let's pinpoint what is common or generic:

First, there is no typical merger. Each one is different. Each stems from different stimuli and motivations. As a result, each causes its protagonists to act differently.

Each M&A starts with an idea in one man's or woman's head. Sometimes, it's impulsive and probably just as often the idea has sat there perking away in that individual's brain for awhile until something else—another event, shift in market share and most likely an M&A involving competitors—catapults that idea into action.

But that idea is infectious. It is rare indeed that only one person comes up with an idea that no one else has or has had. Whether it's due to something contagious wafted along in the air or not, it's highly probable that the idea of buying or selling is occurring simultaneously to two or more people. This could be caused by the same stimuli I described just above, a triggering event that gives birth to the same idea or instinct in more than one individual at the same time.

Want a theory? There's something electric or extra-sensory or kinetically communicative about ideas. I've seen it happen at meetings when two people, sitting apart from one another, erupt with the same idea. They stare at one another in a blend of embarrassment and annoyance. How dare you steal—steal?—my idea? they seem to be asking. But it was really something else such as a simple, identical reaction to the discussion that both heard or participated in.

At the last moment or just before the papers are signed, everyone has remorse. What are they giving up? What are they getting into? Is it a well-thought-out plan? What's the real upside, downside? Suddenly, as either the buyer or seller's hand poises over the merger agreement, an associate whispers something into his or her ear and the hand freezes. Suddenly, the player or players are not so sure. The idea that appeared so right suddenly isn't.

Some of that remorse may be due to the immediate depreciation in the value of the transaction the moment immediately after the papers are signed. What causes it? Uncertainty about the outcome of the deal, uncertainty about imminent and future interest rates and inflation, and, perhaps most important, a loss of interest in a done deal.

When Is It A Merger and When Is It an Acquisition?

When is it a merger and when is it an acquisition? Here's where some of the quirks of human nature prevail. Besides the technical differences, involving a pooling of interest or financial arrangement, here's the difference as M&A people claim. The people in the buying company, which may actually have merged with the other, usually say in the boastful way of the buyer, "We acquired them." But the people in the acquired company say, "We merged with them." If you think that this switching of true situations is contradictory, perhaps you are, to put it most delicately, not fully cognizant of the intricacies of human nature.

Does "no" on an M&A mean "no"? Not really. Never say or think "no, now and forever." "No" can just as easily mean a "delayed yes." As Peter Solomon describes a recent "Perils of Pauline" transaction, "We couldn't sell the client company. We couldn't find anyone really interested. They almost ran out of money. But then, when we had just about given up, a company that had rejected the deal came back out of the woodwork and said it would pay the price that it had rejected. That's rare but it does happen." So be careful about saying or accepting "no" regardless of what side you are on. It could cost you money, if not embarrassment.

Now, let's review a typical American merger—not really typical because each one is so different, but an actual one that has enough characteristics and quirks to render it more or less average. The data comes from a prominent investment banker, who asks to remain unnamed as he works with the three principal companies involved. So, we'll call the banker "Hunt & Find, Inc."; the seller, "Jones Corporation"; and the two competing bidders, "Smith & Company" and "Brown Enterprises." One partner did the principal negotiating for Hunt & Find, Inc. and we'll call him "Ronnie Sharp." We'll be quoting him from time to time. This, I repeat, is a real-life story with just some of the details fudged.

An American Saga, with a Moral

It is a balmy spring morning as Ronnie Sharp, a youngish partner at Hunt & Find, one of New York's most successful venture capital and merger-acquisition specialists, gazes out the window and visualizes how sweet it would be in his boat whipping through Long Island Sound. He's not unhappy, just a workaholic with a love of the outdoors being stirred by the wisps of spring. His intercom rings. It's his boss.

"Ron, I just got a call from a guy named Jones who runs a successful family business," says the boss. "He says he might want to sell. Can you fly down to Baltimore this afternoon?"

At 2:30 that afternoon, Ronnie is sitting in the office of the namesake of Jones Corporation. Jones has no concern about being candid right off. "My old man started this business almost a half-century ago," he said. "Frankly, it's been a money machine for the whole family and we've got a big family. For the last 15 years, since the old man passed on, I've been working like a dog. Now I think I want out. I want to spend more time with my family, especially while the kids are still young. And I want to ski more and sail my yacht a lot more. Ronnie, your boss told me you're a sailor, too, so you know what I mean, don't you?"

Swallowing as he recalls his own wishful lapse that morning, Ronnie asks, "Isn't there anyone else in the family to take over?"

"No one's interested. They all went into different fields early on. It's been just me and the professionals I hired. But I must be up front with you. We are talking to other investment bankers, too."

"I appreciate your honesty. But I think you will find that we know our business."

"This is not an urgent or pressure-driven sale. We can take our time to do it right."

Over the next few weeks, Jones came to Hunt & Find's New York offices, speaking at length to Ronnie, his boss and several associates. Primarily, he wanted to know if they thought his business was salable, what price it might bring, who the most likely buyers might be and what fees Hunt & Find would charge at the outset and at the time of sale. Ronnie also interviewed him again in Baltimore and was told again that Jones was spending some time with competitive M&A people.

About two months after their first meeting, Jones called to say that he had selected Hunt & Find to be his financial advisor in the sale. Ronnie, his boss and an associate flew down to Baltimore as a group and were given the complete financial and operating data on the Jones Corporation. Back home, they analyzed the material. Two weeks later, they flew south again and told Jones that on the basis of the data that he had supplied he could expect between $60 million and $80 million for his company. At that meeting, the group compiled a list of 12 potential buyers. Two or three were considered the most likely to make an offer while one was a dark horse who could either come in and take the Jones Corporation or not come in at all.

That same afternoon, they reviewed all the potential bidders with Jones. The four agreed that the most likely was the Smith Corporation, a larger but similar company. Jones said he knew Smith's chairman, liked him, considered him aggressive and thought that the two companies could marry happily.

At that point, Jones officially hired Hunt & Find, paying a retainer of about $85,000. That amount would be subtracted from the final fee if the investment banker could sell the Jones firm. The fee arrangement was 1-$^1/_2$ percent of any fee up to $80 million or 3 percent if the price went over $80 million. Jones and the bankers then signed an "engagement" letter, which stated that Hunt & Find was Jones' financial advisor for the purpose of selling the business and also set forth the fee arrangement.

Over the next few weeks, Ronnie and several associates worked to assemble all possible information from Jones' senior executives in order to prepare a "book" about the company. This process is known as "due diligence." The point of this, said Ronnie Sharp, was "to raise the skirts a little on the Jones business so we can show it to the potential bidders." But a new element now entered the picture since the outside was now being let in on what was transpiring.

Tension was the new element. Surprisingly, there had been little during the period when Hunt & Find was competing with other firms to get the Jones' assignment. Now there was a risk that the strategic information might fall into the wrong hands. But before a bidder is allowed to receive the data book, its management must sign a confidentiality agreement. It requires the signers not to divulge the name of the firm being sold and asks them to agree not to seek to hire any of the selling firm's executives. "There are some firms that won't sign such an agreement," Ronnie says, "and if they won't we walk away."

But even before the data book is completed or the confidentiality agreement presented, Hunt & Find has already begun calling the 12 potential bidders on its list. Mostly, the call will be placed directly to the chief executive officer. "Usually I tell the CEO who I am and that I represent the Jones Corporation," Ronnie says. "Then I say that I have an acquisition proposal to present. Of course, I have to use my judgment. Normally, the

CEO will take my call immediately or, if unable to, will call me back in 10 minutes. Sometimes, though, I get bucked to the vice president for mergers and acquisitions. But that's rare. Corporate America understands a merger. It's got an urgency and importance of its own."

Now Ronnie Sharp does not call Smith Corporation first, even though it was generally agreed that Smith was the "most likely." The reason: "We want to practice first with someone else," says Ronnie. "We don't want Smith to ask us the impossible questions like, 'Have you talked to any other interested parties?' or 'What price has already been offered for the business?' We don't want to lie, because you can get tangled up in it and it does catch up with you. But it's smart to talk to others first, whether you will be asked or not. It's always good to have a competitive atmosphere when we finally do talk to Smith."

Usually the chief executive approached will respond, "Yes, sounds interesting. Come to see me and tell me about it." Or "I'll be in New York soon and I'll drop over to your office." In either case, Ronnie will ask the CEO to sign the confidentiality agreement and then present the "book."

It is now somewhere between six and eight weeks since Ronnie first met with Jones of Jones Corporation. It is time to approach Smith. "I tell CEO Smith at the start that there are others looking at the property," Ronnie says. "But she's smart. She can see right through me. She knows, even though I don't name the others, that she's the best possible buyer for Jones. She doesn't even need for me to identify the others. She probably knows them immediately or will in short order. She probably knows those potential bidders better than we do."

All the contacts have now been made, including the "dark horse." It's Brown Enterprises, a firm even larger than Smith and said to be better-heeled. Yet, despite all the communications, nothing much has leaked out. The contacts so far are airtight. There are no rumors out there. The Jones' stock is still unruffled.

Within the next week, all potential bidders are surveyed on the extent of their interest. Only four of the 12 stay in, of which Smith appears to be the most certain and Brown still a dark horse. Now it's time for all four semi-finalists to sit down with

Jones' senior management. "I prepared all the Jones people on the type of questions they would probably be asked," Ronnie said, "and also I supervised the assembling of the most wanted information and documents for the bidders."

A "data room" is set up, with a number of files containing all the data, leases, titles and deeds. An index is also made available of all that the room contains. The door is kept locked. But when one of the bidders or its representative is allowed in, a Jones' representative sits in to monitor and record what documents are copied by what bidder.

While this process goes on, two other activities are being carried on. Hunt & Find is now also talking to another layer of potential bidders, those not considered prime candidates but yet companies that might be interested in Jones. And Jones' lawyers are busily drafting a merger agreement, leaving the line blank that is labeled "buyer." The goal of the latter is that an agreement should be readily available in the event a deal is suddenly hammered out.

Separating the Real Bidders from the Wannabees

The next step, taken a week or two later, is intended to separate the real bidders from the wishful thinkers. Each of the four bidders is asked by Hunt & Find to express interest formally by stating a price range that it would pay for the Jones business, how it would plan to pay—whether by cash, stock or bank loan. Also, would the bidder want to acquire by buying the assets or the stock?

These declarations are intended to make the bidder's interest legal and to protect Jones in case there is a dispute later on price or on how the money will be obtained.

At this point, the bidders go home and analyze all the data and decide from it whether they remain interested and, if so, what their offering price range will be and how they plan to pay it.

Now, after two-and-a-half to three months, it's push-and-shove time.

"We go to each bidder," Ronnie says, "and ask 'where are you in this process?' One will say, 'Moderately in, but we are interested only in this part or that part of the company.' We say, 'Thank you but we are interested only in selling the whole business.' We press those still in the game on price. One says, 'We will offer $50 million.' We say, 'Not enough but we may come back to you.' Now we go to the two that are left, Smith and Brown. Smith says, 'I'll give you $80 million in our stock.' Brown says, 'I'll give you $100 million in cash.'

"What do we do next? We tell both Smith and Brown that their offers are a little low," Ronnie Sharp says, "We tell that to Brown even though its price is a very nice one. But we know from experience that no one offers the best price up-front. So we add, 'But we want to talk further.'"

So Smith and Brown are definitely on the hook and Jones of Jones is getting excited as are Ronnie and his colleagues. Both bidders come back with requests for further "due diligence." Hunt & Find keeps up the prodding process as a sense of climax begins to build up. Final offers now come in, each one sweetened from the prior one. Smith has raised its offer to $85 million in stock and Brown is offering $105 million in cash.

Hunt & Find huddles with Jones of Jones. What considerations is Smith offering to Jones if they make the deal? As a big shareholder in Smith, possibly its largest with the stock payout, how much control will Jones have? "Will I be on the board?" he asks. "They haven't said that yet, have they? I'll be left in ski country with no input or clout unless I'm on the board."

But there's a bigger question on Jones' mind. Smith's stock deal is tax-free—that is, until he sells the stock. But Brown's cash offer is subject to a 30 percent capital gains tax. On the other hand, Smith's deal would mean investing the entire $85 million in Smith stock, putting all Jones' eggs in Smith's basket. Now, they agree, Brown's offer is starting to look pretty good. After the capital gains bite, Brown's bid would amount to $75 million in cash which could be partly invested in the good Smith stock and the rest could be invested elsewhere, banked or used to buy, say, a ski resort.

What's the next move?

"We tell them both that we have a competing offer," says Ronnie, "and how much it is. Smith is very annoyed when I tell her that the other bid is higher, and tells me, 'You're lying.' I say, 'Ms. Smith, I never lie because I don't want to get a reputation for lying. It catches up with you.'"

But, Ronnie Sharp adds, "Smith still doesn't believe me. So I tell her that we will keep the auction open for a few more days, in case she wants to raise her bid. By the way, I also tell Brown the same thing." In the meantime, Jones' lawyers are literally breaking their necks to finish the merger agreement so it will be ready for the rapidly approaching deadline.

The process from start to finish has taken a full six months. Hunt & Find, as it awaits final bids, is working with the Jones Corporation's senior officers to arrange employment agreements, as well as nailing down agreements that will serve to continue the business under a new ownership so that, as Ronnie put it, "it won't hit a pothole 8 or 9 months down the road when we can't help it."

Brown Enterprises wins the Jones Corporation with a slightly higher bid of $107 million and is delighted to have won. Jones is happy, making all sort of plans for the future. But Smith of Smith is very unhappy. She just couldn't believe that Brown Enterprises had paid as much as it did. "What made me think you were lying?" she asks Ronnie. "Everyone lies, don't they?"

Not long afterward, the Smith jet flew two of its senior officers to New York to see Ronnie Sharp. They told him, "You got under Smith's skin when she found out that you really didn't lie. But she thinks that Hunt & Find got a very good price and thinks you are very smart. And good negotiators. She wants to hire your firm to see if she can sell her business at a good price too."

chapter 6

It's a Circus; It's an Auction; It's—a Merger

Do you recall the last time you went to the circus? You reacted with pulse-thumping excitement to the frantic montage, no matter what your age was. There was the great sense of luxuriating in a fantasy in the midst of mundane reality. Well, in some real measure, that's the merger scene today. Three, four or five rings of simultaneous action, of feint and foray, good intentions often gone wrong, good intentions gone right, of moves inside and outside other moves, the whole framework hanging on a thin strand of logic and a heavy strand of hope.

Like the small circus at Borden Inc., where Kohlberg, Kravis & Roberts, the leveraged-buyout banker, had apparently gotten approval to buy the old consumer foods company. But a 39-year old, former chief executive of the Sunbeam-Oster Company, Paul B. Kazarian, kept noisily flopping Borden's tent, wanting in. Kazarian wanted to elbow KKR aside, take over the troubled Borden and correct its "chronic mismanagement." Offering to inject $200 million more into the deal, Kazarian invited Borden's directors to a meeting but not one of them showed up.

Like Continental Corporation, a well-established insurer, which thought that it had a done deal with an investment group that would plunk down $275 million for a 20 percent stake in the firm. The cash inflow would have been a comfortable cushion for Continental's cash flow. But along came CNA Financial Corporation, another large insurer, which offered $1.1 billion to take over the entire Continental business. Continental took that deal. To keep everyone happy, Continental agreed to pay $19.6 million in breakup fee and expenses to the unsuccessful investors, Insurance Partners. And, in the same but more expensive vein, CNA agreed, too, to invest $275 million in Continental to replace what the earlier investors promised. Everyone was happy, except for Richard M. Haverland, who was to head Continental under the previous deal.

Or like Pace Membership Warehouses, one of the few remaining, smaller chains of membership warehouse clubs, which decided to sell its 39-store business to diversification-hungry Kmart Corporation, the huge discounter. But Kmart fell into some serious setbacks itself, partially because it allowed its diversity to distract it from its core business to keep up with the Wal-Mart Stores' steamroller. Three years after its Pace acquisition, Kmart launched a divestiture program, selling some of its lagging Pace division to Wal-Mart stores. It was an ironic twist for Pace, which evidently decided it couldn't compete with the two big discounters but wound up being successively owned by both of them.

There were other odd deals. In a historic event, pilots, employees, executives and British Airways assumed control of UAL Corporation, creating the nation's biggest employee-owned company. Total price: more than $7 billion. Now employees who have characteristically complained about the inanities of management would run the airline themselves and choose its management. Can employees hack it as owners? Only time will answer that.

Ralston Purina, the big grain and pet food packer, bought the Beech-Nut Nutrition Company for $85 million. Evidently the buying company hoped that mothers would forget that Beech-Nut was convicted a few years earlier for selling watered-down apple juice for tots. Mothers are generally very kind but how long a memory do they have when it comes to their children?

Each Deal Is a Unique Equation of Cause and Effect

All these are merely an iota of the mergers, acquisitions and divestitures which have been roiling American business in the last few years. Each one is a distinct, perhaps unique equation of cause and effect, of good intentions confronting frustration, of human struggle pitted against difficult, sometimes onerous market forces. But the total—the movement, the flux, the effect on local economies and local people—can be seen as a sort of circus, lots going on in concentric circles. Isn't this—no nasty implication intended—the new American way of doing business?

Across the country, it resembles nothing less than an infectious binge. Takeovers, friendly, hostile or otherwise. One company does it. Seeing it, another follows suit. A third sees it, too, and does likewise. A fourth and fifth—how many in one day? Dozens, you can be sure.

What we are witnessing is an acceleration in the rate of consolidations, patently the newest (and the oldest) form of business strategy. In fact, if one traces in broad strokes the behavior of American business since World War II, it resembles a trajectory from industrial recovery to expansion to product innovation to global expansion to recycling, reengineering, downsizing and now restructuring. Normally, each of these would last at least a decade. But such are the pressures and the challenges that we are telescoping each phase, contracting it in our haste to prepare ourselves for new market positions domestically and internationally. Each instance, raising its own questions of logic and common sense, creates its own suspense.

Are the players mostly shooting dice? Yes, of course. Are their chances of consummating a successful marriage reasonable? Yes, of course. But one can only stand back a bit agog at the frenzy and gyrations of it all. It's—the merger circus.

It's a circus full of flubs, misjudgments, inadequate preparations and too often an inability to understand simple human relationships. Perhaps that is why so many M&As fail. And lots of them do fail. McKinsey & Company, the management consulting company, tracked mergers and found that in a 10-year period only 23 percent of mergers recovered the costs involved in the deals and achieved their synergistic claims. Put another way, that means that 77 percent failed to recover their costs. Is it the circus—the very energy, congestion and heedless enthusiasm—that is responsible? No, I think it's the human error that is the culprit.

Nine Guidelines for Handling a Merger

The nine suggestions that follow are a combination of what merger experts tell me and what I have experienced. Maybe it will recast the circus into a pleasant, tuneful, musical comedy.

1. You have to bring gifts to soothe the unwilling beast, soften any resentment, palliate the fear. The objective is to turn indecisiveness and concern into "well, I don't know, maybe it will be okay, maybe even better." Gifts, a premium over the market price in an M&A, are fine. But it's smart to soften up the company's directors and bankers as well as management and investors. It makes sense to approach them with a direct, face-to-face frankness. The message, in effect, is this: "Listen, I'm the right person for your great company. I care. Check me out." I don't think that's naive.

2. Take time with the merger—what's your rush? This is so obvious as to not require much elaboration. It makes sense to ponder a situation about to be entered into. Get someone else's opinion, making sure that you aren't tipping your hand to a potential rival. It's sensible to see a situation from someone else's perspective because it enables you to see your own more clearly. I know some merger makers who get their kicks from making one deal after another, from the circuslike atmosphere this produces in and around their firms and the notoriety they draw.

3. Keep your human relations clean, clear, neat. Candid, up-front and frequent communications are vital. Speaking honestly will spare you lots of anguish later. That's the case, too, in regard to employee relations of both the acquiring and acquired companies. Nothing is more disturbing to both executives and the rank-and-file than the possibility that they may lose their jobs, suffer an income cut, have to give up some perks or benefits or be thrown into a new, alien culture. Take pains to calm the troubled waters. If you don't, the new structure will be badmouthed just to get even.

4. Do your homework well. It's been established by now that normal "due diligence" won't produce the information a merger-minded company needs. It should insist on being allowed to make its own accounting or audit. Financial information is only part of the game. You need input on marketing, merchandising, competition and a whole host of culture and employee information. Hire experts, even private eyes, if need be. Whoever said that it isn't a good idea to "check out" a potential target company or have it done for you through friends or professionals? Have your human resources people used recruiters to check out the internal culture, morale, behavior of the target company, as if just looking for good recruits? Why not?

5. What do the suppliers think of the target company? As every sales executive and salesman will insist, no one knows more about the inside of a business than those who sell to it, especially if there has been a long-term relationship. The sharpest consultants and recruiters shine up to suppliers to get an inside look at their customers. Of course, there's always the risk of tipping your hand but if you research it diplomatically, the risk is minimized. Let's face it: a supplier who wants to stay in business and grow must develop a keen intelligence system, however informal it is.

6. Be very careful of (1) Wall Street analysts, (2) the media, (3) friends and relatives, the latter whether we are referring to a family or business relationship. Use plain common sense about what you tell them. Unfortunately, analysts have a dual loyalty, one to their industry clients, the other to their employers.

Given a choice what to do with certain information, they will surely tell their employers and possibly their clients; there's nothing illegal about it as long as it isn't insider information being used for profit. As for the media—I am treading on thin ice here. Always remember that there really isn't any such thing as off-the-record. Even if the reporter agrees to hold something confidential, he or she is often subject to sometimes very demanding bosses. What about friends and relatives? Should you confide intimate knowledge of family or business to them? Don't even think about it.

7. **Don't assume that *your* employees should be the ones retained.** This happens all too often so that good people in an acquired company are fired, overlooked or allowed to wander off. Isn't that the old Roman technique of "rewarding" the victorious gladiators and of killing or enslaving the vanquished? That's old stuff and doesn't make a lot of sense anymore. The fact is that if the acquired company is any good—and it has to be pretty good to be attractive—it's probably due to the fact that it employed good people, whether at the top, middle or bottom, who should be retained.

8. **Act similarly with policies, assets, practices and methods.** Don't sweep them aside in favor of those you brought with you. Being bigger or the buyer doesn't guarantee superiority. Too often, however, that attitude dominates takeover behavior. Later, it develops, what was discarded might well have been kept. In mergers, it's axiomatic that frequently insufficient study has been made of the acquired company's properties and practices even after the merger; the "winner takes all" idea flavors all decisions. But it isn't easy as the "winners" furiously try to cut costs to pay for the takeover. After all, throwing out the baby with the bathwater is the easiest way to go but does it make sense?

9. **Be a leader, not a dictator.** This is my last bit of gratuitous advice on how this frenzied circus can be slowed down. The success of M&As depends greatly on the behavior, expression and actions of the people at the top of the combined company. A statesmanlike attitude and especially judicious performance will go a long way to make a merger work. A dollop of

philosophy helps, too. In acquiring a new company, the right attitude might be: "This is a new company. Let's work together to make it succeed, no matter whether you come from the buyer or the seller. We can use every bit of talent and dedication you can give us and we will reward it." That's a tough proposition. Is it platitudinous? Of course. But it just might do the trick and cut down the percentage of M&As that fail.

Seven Abuses the M&As Invite

Even if cut down, the circus won't be over. First, because within so much flurry there's only a small chance that the same mistakes that so many consolidations bring won't be repeated. Second, because our natural drive to expand a business inevitably leads us to buy more, to swallow up the competition or, failing that, to sell what we have. That's human nature, in the raw. So the riders whirl around in a madcap race, scarcely avoiding a collision, sending up clouds of dust, as we stare wide-eyed.

It also isn't over—because there's yet something more which sustains it. Shenanigans.

Shenanigans? M&As lend themselves to it. My reporting and research over the years have found that there are seven different types of abuses—illegal or immoral or both—that keep the merger game in a constant whirl. They are as follows:

1. Executives who decide to sell a company turn greedy because they stand to gain materially from the sale. This becomes a conflict of interest.

The buyers hold out some shiny plums to the sellers—juicy contracts, lucrative retirement plans, lush golden handshakes, other great perks. They do all this and more to get the decision makers to agree to the sale and to continued employment if they prefer. Sadly, many an otherwise decent, honest executive has stepped over the line trying to decide between reasonable salary and employment benefits and excessive inducements. I recall one top executive who swore to me that as a member of the board of his company he would pound on the conference table and inveigh against a buyout offer from a rival company.

But when the time came, he didn't do that at all. No one on his side did, including the CEO. The 10 members of the board, sharing a pot of $50 million in golden handshakes, voted to approve the deal.

2. Shareholders in takeover deals usually take a back seat to management which gives its own interests top priority.

Is this one of those "needless to say" matters? I hope not. First, it's a fact that shareholders often are as much at fault as management because they tend to sit by silently when the merger feelers begin, especially when the business and profit trends are good and the stock is performing well. Second, top management in too many cases has little feeling, respect or consideration for the shareholders, however warmly and differently they express their sentiments. But the fact is that shareholders do have real clout if they can band together to express themselves and do so with the right timing.

3. The theft of trade secrets, embezzlement, and even sabotage are always possible because of the insecurity and unfulfilled expectations so typical of many mergers and acquisitions.

It's a fact that quite a few executives of acquired companies soon leave because of disillusionment, disappointment, and frustration with the new management. Others hang on, feathering their own nests or just digging in, while others use their jobs as a base to make additional income, and still others will cross over into illegal activities. The litigation over such acts has grown steadily over the years. Trade secrets are valuable information.

4. Ethical problems easily arise in takeovers with deferred payment or contingency arrangements with the seller.

Ultimate payment to the seller is often based on the acquired company's future earnings under the new owner. Sometimes the pressure to produce earnings prompts acquired executives to load up capital expenditures in order to produce short-term results at the expense of long-term needs. But the buying company's brass can be just as tricky and devious. They can saddle the new subsidiary or division with big overhead charges, management fees and other financial burdens so as to cut back the acquired company's earnings. If you're skeptical, don't be. It has happened. But these maneuvers on either side resemble a double-edged sword. No one wins.

5. "Looking for Mr. Right (or Even Wrong)." This can be as a white-knight bolting into the melee of a hostile takeover or just sauntering through the front door because of an invitation.

Why is a white knight courted? The common denominators in controversial tender offers that fuel such invitations from unhappy directors, shareholders, overambitious company executives, hyperactive company finders and a financial whiz with a thyroid disorder are plainly unhappiness, overzealousness, selfishness or old-fashioned avarice, either singly or in combination. There's always the hope that the company under the White Knight instead of the one making the initial pitch will produce a new environment, preferably one that rewards the intelligence imparted by the person or persons who rang the new owner's bell. But all too often such intrigues fail to produce. Still, bringing in a white knight to foil an attacker is acceptable as long as it doesn't lead to special deals with those who summon him (or her).

6. If the role of stockbrokers and officers of large financial institutions becomes overaggressive, it can easily disrupt a company from pursuing its chosen course and put it into "play."

It's the old story of a company whose parts are worth more than the whole or whose value has been unfairly discounted by investors. The game then works like this: Rolling the cursor up and down a computer screen, an investment banker, a Wall Street analyst or bank employee finds an undervalued stock which looks like it could fly. Then that person or someone delegated visits the management of the company with the sleeper stock and suggests ways in which the company could capitalize on its potential. If the management is stubborn and insists that its current direction is best, the touter could then go to an acquisition-minded company or merger player and suggest the stubborn company as a likely takeover pigeon. Meanwhile, the touter is probably buying shares of the potential target, either personally or for clients, getting ready to make a killing once the company is actually approached for a takeover.

So far, the only possible illegality that has occurred in this entire process is that of insider trading. A professional investor, a banker, an analyst or whatever can be tagged only if he or she buys shares on the basis of official information received but not imparted to all shareholders. But—go prove it. It's tough enough for the Securities and Exchange Commission to do it.

7. Which brings us more or less naturally to the winner's and loser's complex that underlies every merger or acquisition. It's probably the most overriding reason for personal misbehavior in business takeovers.

So who actually wins or loses in the merger game? Can it possibly be both—or neither? On the surface, everyone involved tends to insist that good intentions and honest dealings are the norm in the business of buying and selling companies. And it's impossible to predict at the outset who will win and who will lose because of all the unknowables that lurk in the future. These take time to develop. They include the future turns of the company's fortunes, its image, the efficiency of the combined company's management, the degree or lack of duplication of manpower, physical and other assets between the owning company and its newly acquired unit. That's what everyone tells you for any public consumption.

But privately, what the players say will be a different story as it often is in business—if you're lucky enough for them to let you in on it.

Like what? Like such covert problems as private debt, or superannuated inventory, or covered-up and inflated expenses of the seller or the buyer, or whether the buyer will use the assets of the acquired company strictly for the benefit of the merged company or for some ulterior, evil purpose, or what will be done with the pension fund of the acquired company. This list could go on quite a while. But such potential abuses will help to determine more often than not who the winner and loser will be, corporately or privately. The senior executives in either a buying or selling company may also be responsible if anyone or a group working for them is committing or has committed fraud or embezzlement.

So many court suits have been filed alleging such crimes in the wake of a merger that one can easily assume that every M&A has a criminal side. But this is not true at all. However, all the players and investors in a merger should be vigilant and curious about all the goings-on.

Such court cases generally fall into two categories. One concerns the effort by someone or several people to induce others to help them to take over a target company. This can involve illegal payments, promises of well-paying jobs, offers of lush perks such as cars, boats, even homes, not to mention expensive cruises and vacations. The government must prove not only the fact but the intent to defraud. The other general abuse seems to arise from disenchanted executives who carry out their frustration in one or more illegal ways.

The company man or woman who used to practically profess loyalty out loud before the takeover sometimes becomes bitter, unfulfilled and disgusted because promises expected to be very favorable are not delivered. Once thoroughly disillusioned, everything else seems to fit the abusive pattern, including work given or not given, lack of respect, and raises that go to others. The disgruntled employee starts thinking about getting even and there are many ways to do that, ranging from theft and selling trade secrets to arson.

So much for shenanigans. Let's explore some other "rings" in the circus.

Tracking Down the Real Players

One of the other elements that give M&As their energy is their mobility. They begin at one stage, progress through several more, seem to stumble into some more and then are concluded or dropped. The process can be fast or slow but it is a moving one.

They're not at all like other business newsmakers. Senior management appointments are usually static affairs, consisting perhaps of an advance telephone call and then a publicity release which is normally cryptic, antiseptically clean (the board of directors had to check it out first, right?),and always lacking in detail. But it's just a one- or two-shot. Financial reports are about the same. Dividend releases at the most draw a yawn. New products are a little more exciting, offering a little more drama but are essentially narrow in significance and limited in motion.

Mergers and acquisitions, though, are full of action and drama, not to mention suspense. They are the closest thing in financial journalism to a good ball game. Although I've missed my share, I'd like to tell you about a few that I've covered, ferreted out and helped to bring to public consciousness before the principals were quite ready. Not that I am the world's greatest investigative reporter. But I was only a determined journalist who, when working on the *New York Herald Tribune* and then on the *New York Times*, got a particular kick out of breaking stories. Merger-acquisition stories were the most exciting to me because of their intrinsic drama and the fact that everyone was trying to keep them under wraps until all the t's were crossed and the i's dotted.

In one case, the Federal Trade Commission said that it would allow two substantial firms to merge providing that the larger one would dispose of its midwest subsidiary. This provision, intended to remove any possibility of unfair competition, was announced by both companies and the senior one then set about selling off the subsidiary. The financial press then competed to unearth who would buy it or had already bought it. What made it especially interesting was that the subsidiary about to be disposed of was the real profit-maker in the company. Yet, the latter was anxious enough to make the deal even if it had to sacrifice its best asset.

No one in either company was talking and we were all at a dead end in tracking it down. It was about the third day after the original announcement that I came into the *Times* newsroom and decided that I would break that story that day. Starting about 10 a.m. I phoned all the standard sources— industry regulars, Wall Street analysts, a couple of consultants who had their antennae wired into the industry. Nothing.

By the afternoon, I was beginning to feel frustrated. I was certain there were anywhere from six to 10 other newspaper people, not to mention analysts, consultants and recruiters trying to dig the story out, too, all for their own purposes. But I wasn't getting anywhere. Then I got a brainstorm. What companies would be the most likely ones to buy it? Why don't I try them? They would deny it, of course, but maybe a morsel would inadvertently drop from their lips. So I called. The first two knew about the agreement to sell that company but insisted they weren't interested and weren't involved. Then I tried the third company, speaking to someone I knew there.

"No, it's not us," he said. "They did talk to us but we told them we've got too many other things on our plate."

"Oh. So who are they talking to now?"

"Don't know. But I hear it's somebody in the South."

Wow! The South. What's that—12 states? Well, I told myself, that's better than 50. That's narrowing it down, right? In the next hour, I kept the phone hot and my colleagues sitting near me got interested. That hunt-and-find game can become very infectious. Finally, at almost 4:30, I spoke to someone who told me, cryptically, "Whyn't yo-all check out Little Rock?"

"Little Rock!" I yelled. "Of course, of course. Little Rock's as good as any other place! Why the heck not?"

Now my colleagues started clustering around me. I reached someone I knew in that city. He said, "Look, I shouldn't tell you but I will. Try Stephens & Company. They're the investment bankers down here and they're damned ambitious."

Wow once more! Stephens & Company. I had vaguely heard of that company but I didn't recall in what context. When I phoned Stephens' office in Little Rock, I simply asked for "Mr. Stephens." "Which one?" the receptionist asked. "The boss, the man in charge," I said. "Oh, you mean Jim Stephens?" "I guess so." "I'm sorry, sir, but he's not here." I was getting a little rocky from telephonitis by then. "Where is he when he's not here?" I asked weakly. "You'll find him at the country club," she said.

So I tried Jim Stephens on the golf course, in the lounge and at the bar. No Jim Stephens. As a last resort, I asked the switchboard, "Do you think he might be in the locker-room?" "Could be. I'll put you through." The locker-room phone rang a few times until a voice of indiscriminate age said, "Hello." I said, "I'd like to talk to Jim Stephens. Is he there by any chance?"

"This is Jim Stephens. I'm standing here in a towel, I'm soakin' wet from the shower, so what in hell do you want?"

"Mr. Stephens, I'm checking out a report that your company is buying the midwest subsidiary of—"

Silence. "Who did you say this is?" Stephens asked.

I told him and then I repeated the question. Now here's where Jim Stephens stepped into history and earned himself the right to be a charter member of The-I-Only-Talk-Honest to the Press-Hall-of-Fame. "I can't tell you that," he said. "But I will tell you that—I think you are a pretty damned good reporter."

Well, I made the first edition with that story by the skin of my teeth, with my colleagues pounding me on the back and we beat the competition cold.

End of story? No. To further show you why this merger business is just a circus, the next morning one of the reporters from another department came over to me with a big smile and an outstretched hand. "How the hell did you ever break that story?" he demanded. "My father's in that business and he told me who was buying the company. But it was being kept very hush-hush for a few more days. I couldn't tell you guys in financial about it because Dad got it in total confidence. But he and I were talking about it this morning."

I didn't know whether to punch him on the nose because he had known and wouldn't tell us or shake his hand. I didn't do either. I just said, "Thanks." Now that's the end of the story.

Another time, another place. I was tracking some rumors about a possible merger between a company founded by a retiring genius and another founded by a demanding, loud, tough guy. Mr. Tough Guy had proposed a merger with Mr. Genius but everyone thought it would be a disaster. First of all, the company founded by Mr. Genius was a fine, high-class operation destined to be one of the giants of its field, whereas Mr. Tough Guy's firm had a reputation for so-so quality, high pressure and little customer happiness. The prognosis for such a marriage was not good. But the better firm badly needed a firm administrative hand and that was the reason why Mr. Genius was talking merger to Mr. Tough. So far, the rumors about it had been inconclusive.

One evening, my phone rang. It was Mr. Tough's secretary who said that he wanted to see me right away. "He said to tell you that something important was going on," she said, "and he wanted you to be in on it."

"Are they finally talking about getting together?" I asked.

"Yes," she said, "but please don't ask me."

Twenty minutes later, I was sitting in Mr. Tough's office outside a conference room buzzing with lots of conversation, occasional cursing and reeking of cigars. The suite was ablaze with light, everyone apparently being asked to stay on after regular hours while the deal was being hammered out. After a few minutes, I asked the secretary, "What's going on in there?" She shrugged, "They're still working things out. It's taking longer than we thought. But Mr. T. knows you're here."

Later, I learned there were about 20 people representing both companies. Mr. Tough sat at the head of the table, Mr. Genius at the foot, in what must have been a symbolic precursor of what would eventually happen. There were also lawyers for both camps and, surprisingly, a consulting psychologist. Why he was there I can only guess, but then he was a member of Mr. Tough's board so I concluded that he was really there to watch for kinks in Mr. Genius's makeup for the benefit of Mr. Tough.

An hour later, I was still there. The only change was that Mr. Tough had sent out a platter with a bottle of scotch, some peanuts and a couple of cigars to help me while away the time. But it didn't work. I told the secretary, "I have to leave. Here's my home number. Call me when it's over." A look of horror passed over her pleasant face. "You can't do that. Mr. T. will kill me. Please wait." So I stayed.

But it was slowly dawning on me what was really going on. I was being used. Certainly, I appreciated being summoned and being in a good position to report the event accurately from near first-hand observation. But why call me so early in the day, apparently hours before they expected to shake hands on a deal? I could only conclude that it was because Mr. Tough thought he might get some negotiating mileage from telling them all, "Listen, let's get to a deal here. I got this reporter from the *New York Times* waiting outside to call his office with the story. They think it's important, so dammit let's come to a head here."

Skipping through the next hour-and-a-half, Mr. Tough emerged twice to make sure I was still there and not ready to take off.

About 10:30 p.m., his secretary appeared. "Come," she said, triumphantly. "They're ready for you."

Outside the conference room, Mr. Tough waited with some of his people. "It's all over," he said. "We got a marriage. The shysters are preparing a release for you. Only you will have it, you lucky bastard! Then you can ask us all kinds of questions— and everything will be on the record. But first, I want you to meet someone."

He took me into the conference room and there sat Mr. Genius, pale, inwardly torn, infinitely sad. He knew me vaguely and didn't want to talk to me. But Mr. Tough put the arm on him again. I excused myself to call in and make the last edition. I did a brief interview with both Mr. T and Mr. G and then left. That was well past midnight. But before I turned the corner, I saw the two of them walking along arm in arm, no doubt heading for a local bar so that Mr. T. could give Mr. G. an earful on what should be done from then on and, no doubt, forever.

By the way, the combined company was sold two more times in the next five years and then joined the dustbin of failed mergers.

One more, if you please. I broke a story somewhat later about another big company buying a famous old one, a modern success taking over a traditional business that just couldn't adapt to change. In contrast to the one about the midwest subsidiary, this one took no sweat at all. I lucked into two direct and important sources who independently confirmed the rumor I had been hearing. I wrote the story but it was very routinely handled, because my editors and I didn't know how important it really was. But in the industry the next morning, it produced a bombshell. Sometimes, you learn the most from the reaction of others. We didn't quite appreciate the economic scope, the human drama and the marketing significance of that transaction.

They're all there, those elements, in every business transaction that involves altering the ownership of a business. Each one is a different mix, so that each transaction is *sui generis*, one of a kind.

But when you consider that there are dozens of such unique transactions taking place every single day, then you know why I can call the merger game a circus, a moving montage of people, principles and power. P.T. Barnum would have loved it.

chapter 7

Unfriendly Fire: Hostile Deals and Competing Bidders

For a while, as the 1980s gave its last gasp and the 1990s came in, it really appeared as if the days of the hostile merger had largely faded. After the successive American binges in con-glomerates, leveraged buyouts and junk bonds, everyone seemed to be settling into a kind and gentle mode. But it did-n't last very long.

In a half-dozen megadeals, hostility emerged as one of the cardinal traits of the merger-and acquisition boom of the 1990s.

"Hostility is probably the one clear trend in the merger field in the United States that is different from the recent past," asserts Brian Finn, managing director of the First Boston Corporation, the big New York investment banking house and co-head of its mergers and acquisition practice. "What makes it especially so is the fact that the big, very visible corporations in the United States are involved either in unfriendly takeovers or in trying to break someone else's deal," he said. "I'm talking about the General Electric Company, American Home Products, Union Pacific Corporation, Rockwell International and Browning-Ferris."

He added, in an interview, "These are corporate-to-corporate strategic moves, not just financial deals. They see the big opportunities and even if they have to jump in on someone else's deal, they feel that they have to do it. They have to pursue it."

But Bernard Jacobs, head of Chase Manhattan Corporation's merger-acquisition practice, disagrees that the hostile trend is either large or significant.

"They have a certain romance about them but they are not what the M&A business is about," said Jacobs, in an interview. "Even at their peak in the 1986-1987 period, there were less than 100 and as little as 30 in which the hostile initiator was the victor. In 1994, there will be 4,500 transactions globally with selling prices greater than $10 million that will be completed. But, of them, the number of successful hostile transactions will be less than 50. But they will grab the front pages of newspapers."

One might well interject that it's probably heartening to still see some shoving and jostling, even a little kicking, going on in American business. It demonstrates, if nothing else, that the foreign critics of the United States are dead wrong. We are not impotent, weak and sliding headlong into the ashcan of history. At times, we may seem to be hovering on the brink but we still have some sparks of energy left that could flare into a firestorm anytime.

Four Company Wars

Let's look at four of these brush-wars that took place in recent months:

1. The Santa Fe Pacific Corporation, the large Midwest and Western railroad, accepted in principle a peaceful takeover bid from Burlington Northern Inc., a competitive line, for $3.06 billion in stock. But along came Union Pacific Corporation with a combination cash-and-stock offer, then raised it to $3.28 billion, throwing the earlier deal into complete disarray. Some large Santa Fe shareholders expressed more interest in the new offer than in the old. The issue was tossed into the laps of the Santa Fe directors who could, according to the loose terms of the Burlington Northern arrangement, overturn the tentative without paying the usual "breakup" fee.

Officially, until the directors acted one way or another, Santa Fe management maintained that the deal with Burlington was the superior one. But in a letter faxed to Santa Fe's chief executive officer, Robert Krebs, Union Pacific's president, Richard Davidson, charged that Santa Fe had failed to respond to the better offer. He further told Krebs, "It is not possible for you to consider our proposal fairly without meeting with us."

But Santa Fe did respond. It said it would consider Union Pacific's offer and in the meantime asked its shareholders not to tender their stock to that company. Obviously more in the war of the railroads was to come.

2. Reliance Electric Company, a Cleveland, Ohio industrial equipment producer, also found itself the football between two brawny players. First, it consented to a $1.3 billion stock offer from the General Signal Corporation. Stamford, Connecticut. A provision in the deal would compel Reliance to pay a $50 million breakup fee to General Signal if it signed up instead with another suitor. Then Rockwell International Corporation, a leading maker of aerospace, auto products and industrial automation equipment based in Seal Beach, California, touched off a $1.5 billion tender offer for Reliance stock in October 1994. Rockwell claimed that it had actually beaten General Signal to the punch by approaching Reliance in July and then was shocked when Reliance and General Signal announced their merger in August.

Justifiably, Rockwell's directors were loath to commit themselves on the hostile but higher bid because of the breakup fee. And then in November Rockwell played its ace card by offering to proceed with its tender offer without Reliance needing to sign a formal merger agreement. This was nothing less than a clever ploy to allow Reliance to emerge from its deal with General Signal without needing to pay the breakup fee. In other words, by going directly to Reliance's shareholders, Rockwell wouldn't need a formal merger because it would, if successful, own the majority of stock.

John C. Morley, Reliance's president, was pleased by the new proposal. "It indicates a willingness to address one of Reliance's principal concerns about the Rockwell tender offer," said Morley. He added that his company would "carefully review the terms of any legally binding proposal" submitted by Rockwell.

But the offer had some strings attached. Rockwell president Donald R. Beall said his company wouldn't require a formal deal if Reliance would cancel its "poison-pill" rule aimed at putting off any hostile offer and would also give up some other legal defense measures. And, like the other unfriendly fire, obviously more was to come in this contretemps.

And so it did. After resisting Rockwell for a month, Reliance in November 1994 agreed to be acquired. Rockwell had to sweeten the deal a bit, paying $1.6 billion. The extra $100 million would help Reliance pay the $50 million breakup fee, as well as $5.2 million in expenses to General Signal and then some. In departing the situation, General Signal said that a bidding war would have reduced the savings it had to achieve from the proposed merger. Instead, the money planned to pay for it will be used to make General Signal more efficient and allow it to make "small acquisitions." Rockwell said that the transaction, which creates a $14.5 billion giant equipment maker, will "make us a leading worldwide player in the factory automation business."

3. A bigger breakup fee, amounting to $100 million, was also clouding the air at Kemper Corporation, which had made a deal to be acquired by the Conseco Corporation in preference to the General Electric Company. That sum was the amount that Kemper would have to pay to Conseco if Kemper accepted a better offer. Conseco had outbid General Electric, which withdrew after it decided that the higher Conseco bid wasn't worth matching for Kemper. So, in a great sense—at least to the tune of $100 million—Kemper and Conseco were married to each other, even if the transaction had not yet been completed.

Five months after Conseco's victory but before Kemper shareholders had yet voted on the transaction, Conseco cut back its offer for Kemper by about $29 million. The new offering price was $2.96 billion, down from $3.25 billion, and it brought the price tag down to just about what General Electric had offered. The price scaleback was a rare event. But Conseco explained that since the June agreement in principle its own stock had fallen 26 percent, reflecting investor doubt that the deal would yield the profits that Conseco had originally expected. In a statement, Steven Hilbert, Conseco's chairman, said that he doubted that the company's shareholders would have approved the terms of the original agreement.

For Kemper's shareholders, the 10 percent discount would not be one that they would enjoy. But Conseco was to have the last word. In November, it entirely withdrew its offer for Kemper, citing its own faltering stock price.

4. In an international, hostile campaign that took three months to complete, Browning-Ferris Industries, the American-based, second-largest waste-management company in the world, acquired Attwoods P.L.C. of Slough, England, for $615 million. By winning Attwoods, whose American operations make it the fourth biggest waste management company in the U.S., Browning-Ferris beat out Ikotek Waste Recycling Corporation, a Toronto, Canada waste hauler which actually offered Attwoods more money. But Attwoods didn't take Ikotek's offer seriously, considering it a frivolous offer.

But that wasn't Browning-Ferris' only support. The American company succeeded with its tender offer of 116.75 pence, or $1.83 a share (against Ikotek's 130 pence, or $2.02 a share) because another Canadian hauler, Laidlaw Inc., had previously agreed to sell its 29.8 percent share of Attwoods to Browning-Ferris for 109 pence, or $1.71 a share.

Partly because Ikotek entered the picture only in the final two weeks of the fracas, things became unhinged in general. Browning-Ferris bagged its game, but because of the hostile bid, it never had a chance to conduct a "due diligence" of Attwoods.

So the Americans scheduled a meeting with their new English employee-cousins because, as a Browning-Ferris spokesman put it, "We need a good, detailed picture of what we bought."

Some Earlier Hostilities

Aside from full-page newspaper advertisements that Union Pacific Corporation placed in major newspapers stating its case with unfavorable comparison to Burlington Northern's, the American public has been largely unaware of the fight between rival bidders for some well-known American companies in the 1990s. But it will change if, as some forecasters say, the hostility incidence grows during the rest of the decade.

If so, it may mark a return to the frenzied battling in the 1980s.

Ralph L. Nelson, professor of economics at Queens College of the City University of New York, cites the four major U.S. merger movements prior to the present one: 1897-1902, 1926-1930, 1966-1970 and 1981-1986. Of the last two, he says "there were few hostile takeovers during the 1966-1970 period. But in the next one, from 1981 to 1986, there were many. In both periods, there was an increased role for large companies. In the case of the 1966-1970 period, it was conglomerates. But in the later one, it was large corporations in general."

Over the many years that I was a business writer for the *New York Times*, I recall some exciting fights with unexpected twists.

Some were downright nasty as in the attempt in the early 1970s by The Limited Inc., the Columbus, Ohio women's apparel retailer, to take over Carter Hawley Hale Stores of Los Angeles, now known as Broadway Stores Corporation. After prevailing upon local politicians in California to issue proclamations supporting his company (amid innuendo that "no Los Angeles company will let itself be acquired by some hick outfit") Philip M. Hawley, Carter Hawley's chairman, attracted the General Cinema Corporation to be the "white knight" in the affair. The Limited withdrew (only to try again vainly a few years later) but General Cinema extracted as its fee for intervening a 30 percent chunk of Carter Hawley's stock. Eventually, this became the basis for General Cinema's acquiring all of Carter Hawley's specialty-store businesses, including Neiman Marcus and Bergdorf Goodman, divesting the California company of two of its glitziest jewels.

General Cinema, based in Framingham, Massachusetts, went on to add book publishing to its portfolio by acquiring Harcourt Brace Jovanovich in its biggest purchase and changed its name to Harcourt General Corporation. From the bitter, seven-week Limited-Carter Hawley-General Cinema fracas, the two bidders profited. But Carter Hawley Hale eventually fell into voluntary bankruptcy as it tried to cope with its merger-defense debt and a rapidly eroding California economy. The Limited's chairman, Leslie H. Wexner, swallowed his disappointment and moved on to build his company into a $10 billion apparel dynamo. General Cinema's chairman, Richard Smith, adding fashion retailing to his bottling and movie-theater businesses, savored the taste of consumer-goods diversification and jumped into the book business with both feet. His company is now a highly diversified concern serving varied consumer interests. Carter Hawley emerged from bankruptcy in 1993 after Philip Hawley retired and is now run by a new chief executive.

Will the Hostility Trend Continue?

"It will continue in selected situations, in my opinion," said Laurence S. Grafstein, head of the telecommunications and media practice at Wasserstein Perella & Co., New York investment bankers. "As companies exist in a Darwinian situation where companies are under pressure to expand, hostile M&As will persist. The gloves are off. As institutional investors insist on constant growth in the company they invest in, the easy way to grow is through mergers," he said. "If it takes a hostile effort or a battle with another bidder, then so be it."

Brian Finn of First Boston is also convinced that the trend will sustain itself. "I think that that type of transaction will lead to more of the same," he says. "The very fact that companies of the size and stature of General Electric, American Home

Products and Union Pacific will try to do an unfriendly deal or compete with another company for the right to acquire a third one makes the hostile offer more respectable. Others will follow suit. 'If it's good enough for GE,' they will say, 'it's good enough for me.'"

Steven Wolitzer, co-head of mergers and acquisitions at Lehman Brothers, sees a continuation of hostile deals but most will be friendly ones.

"We're seeing a few hostile moves, not because a lot of American corporations have that tendency," he said. "Neither Rockwell International nor Reliance Electric was unusually aggressive but Rockwell saw a need to move on Reliance for strategic, market share reasons."

Wolitzer does not foresee a resurgence of the "real, financial raider kind of attacks" prevalent in the last two decades because prices of companies are high and defensive mechanisms such as the anti-takeover "poison pill" provisions and the state defense laws are entrenched and strong. "Another element working against hostiles is the fact that nowadays proxy fights are started by institutions such as union pension funds and the like," he says. "They are getting more active in corporate governance."

Hostile transactions are becoming more difficult to carry out because of state actions which have grown in number in the last 10 to 15 years, says Samuel L. Hayes, who holds the Jacob Schiff chair in investment banking at the Harvard Graduate School of Business Administration. "The Clinton administration has taken a 'hand's on' posture in antitrust enforcement but more states are taking action on their own to protect companies domiciled in them. They range from various types of 'poison pills' to strictures such as 80 percent of shares have to be voted in favor of unfriendly offers," said Professor Hayes.

So, bottom line, will the hostiles rate speed up? Yes. How important will it be? Probably not very, unless they become rampant or lead to such megadeals that they will inhibit competition. But it will inject much color and excitement in a business that might otherwise be quite mechanical. Will hostiles be good or bad for American business? It will be good because the attack, threat of it or notice of it will wake up some sleeping companies. It will be bad if it causes an otherwise healthy, thriving company to fall under the heel of a buyer who really wants it more for ego gratification than for strategic reasons. But sometimes it's hard to tell when that buyer first prances through the front door. One shouldn't make too much of either the big smile or the heavy frown. Actions count more.

chapter 8

The Global Clamor for Making Deals

A 37-year-old Saudi Arabian prince, who lives in a 130-room palace in Riyadh, the country's capital, has been eagerly scooping up major stakes in American, Canadian and European business. Prince Walid bin Talal, a billionaire nephew of King Fahd, has been busy, very international in his interests and inclined to pop up in all sorts of places.

In 1991, the gentle-looking prince became Citicorp's largest stockholder when he bought $500 million of the bank holding company's preferred stock which was depressed by bad real-estate loans. In 1993, he acquired about 10 percent of Saks Fifth Avenue, the posh specialty-store retailer. In June 1994, he bailed out a seriously struggling Euro Disneyland near Paris by paying between $400 million and $500 million for a percentage ranging from 13 to 24 percent depending on a stock rights offering. A month later, he bought 50 percent of the Fairmont hotel chain for an undisclosed amount. And in September 1994, he acquired a 25 percent interest in the Four Seasons Hotels, the luxury-oriented Canadian hotel chain, for $122.1 million.

The Saudi-Arabian prince is only the latest foreigner to display interest in buying parts of or entire American, European and Canadian businesses. Other well-known, acquisitive visitors have included Sir James Goldsmith and Robert Maxwell from England, Rupert Murdoch from Australia and Robert Campeau from Canada. But all manner of foreign companies have invested or bought American companies in the last decade. The British Marks & Spencer acquired Brooks Brothers, the traditional American clothing chain. The German Tengelmann food chain bought control of the A&P supermarkets. In moves by two of Japan's leading companies, Sony Corporation acquired CBS Records and Matsushita bought the entertainment empire of MCA Inc. An Australian real-estate developer, the Hooker Company, acquired a number of American retailers and then lost them when the parent company defaulted on its home debts. An Indonesian company bought the business producing Chicken of the Sea tuna, one of America's best-selling brands in that field.

Americans might well have begun to worry if their country wasn't a bargain just waiting to be snapped up. But, within their own and nearby countries, foreign companies have also been busy generating mergers and acquisitions. In Mexico, the lagging Grupo Financiero Inverlat SA recently merged with the much larger Grupo Financiero Serfin SA in a stock exchange, the combination becoming that nation's second biggest financial group. In November 1993, the world's largest paint and industrial-coating producer was created in a $1.73 billion acquisition of the bulk of Nobel Industries A.B., of Sweden, by Akzo N.V., the Netherlands. Canada's largest communications group was established in a March 1994 merger between Rogers Communications and Maclean Hunter Ltd. for $2.5 billion after a bitter, five-week standoff.

It's a Two-Way Street: U.S. Buys Foreign Companies

The United States has been acquiring foreign companies, too, but at a slower pace than it used to. In 1967, American investments represented almost half of the total investment worldwide but they have since dropped to less than a third. However, the latest numbers indicate that foreign investments in the U.S. are growing at a much faster pace than American purchases of foreign companies and are approaching an estimated $1 trillion. By the end of 1995, the Japanese, who have become the most avid buyers of American properties, could be the owners of 10 percent of all U.S. assets. That ownership has also made them the employers of more than 1 million Americans of the more than 3 million employed by foreign firms.

Still, with all the foreign investments in American business, the U.S. hasn't yet sustained the extent of foreign ownership that other major developed countries have. In Great Britain, about one-fifth of all sales were contributed by companies owned by foreigners. Considering Japan's aggressive U.S. takeovers as well as those of the British, who had been the most persistent buyers until the Japanese took over that role, the 20 percent level could be easily reached. The reasons for the shift in movement between the foreigners buying into the U.S. and the U.S. buying foreign are the trade imbalance, which makes American firms open to major investment, and the up-and-down dollar. In a sense, pursuing this thinking, U.S. business is truly a bargain and its managers are eager to sell.

But this might be viewed as simplistic. Foreign businesses praise the American market as the most stable and largest in the world, offering multiple opportunities with its millions of busy shoppers and two-income families. The recession that bridged the 1980s and 1990s was not as great in the U.S. as it was in many other countries, thus building additional confidence among international investors. Ironically, as foreign investors bought in, it seemed to ignite more acquisition interest among others. No one likes being left out of an exciting buying event. There's little doubt, though, that one of the big attractions was the American infrastructure—the banks and investment bankers, the much respected service companies from IBM Corporation to UPS to ARA Services, not to mention AT&T and its two bustling competitors.

But regardless of whatever other reasons the foreign buyers have, nothing can gainsay the gilt-edged worth of many of those acquisitions of Americana such as the long, unbroken span of Los Angeles office-tower skyline that was acquired by the Japanese; the Exxon Building in Rockefeller Center in Manhattan similarly acquired; Celanese Corporation, the big textile producer now owned by the West Germans; Doubleday & Company, one of the major American book publishers, owned by the Germans; Pillsbury flour and other products, now British; and Goldman Sachs, probably Wall Street's most prestigious company, in which a $500 million stake was taken by the Japanese. In other words, the foreign companies have bought some—perhaps much—of the best that we have.

Who's Helping the Foreigners to Buy the U.S.?

It stands to reason that foreign investors aren't just acting on their own. The U.S. is inviting them in three ways.

First, American investment bankers have set up shop in London, Paris and other European cities to act as brokers for nationals eager to buy a chunk of Uncle Sam. Goldman Sachs, for example, was one of the first to do this and remains the most active in helping British business to buy American and also to acquire in the United Kingdom and Europe. Salomon Brothers, another aggressive Wall Street firm, also is helping the Brits. It's not merely advice and use of a computer that these bankers are offering but funds, as well, to make a takeover successful. As far back as 1987, Shearson Lehman Hutton, a once prominent Wall Street house then owned by American Express Company but now dispersed into other firms, put up some of the money for the Beazer Company, a British construction firm, to make a hostile bid for the Koppers Company of Pittsburgh, Pennsylvania.

Second, American companies are often eager to attract foreign overtures as a means of solving their financial and competitive problems. It's not much different from the growing practice of certain industrially-depressed areas of the U.S. to seek foreign investment in order to stimulate the regional economy and create jobs. This was particularly true of certain southern and western states. But corporate efforts to bring in a foreign parent are sometimes a way of fending off a hostile tender by a domestic rival. A few years ago, Chesebrough-Pond's was being stalked by American Brands, Inc., an ambitious, domestic competitor. Fearing that it might be ultimately folded into the other company and disappear altogether. Chesebrough Pond's attracted Unilever, the huge British-Dutch conglomerate, to make an offer and promptly accepted a $3.1 billion bid.

Why would an American company prefer a foreign to a domestic owner? Obviously, as in the Chesebrough case, it was a way of surviving in contrast to being swallowed up by an aggressive rival. But more often, it's because foreign ownership, particularly British and Dutch, offers a gentler, more hands-off relationship than could be expected from a domestic owner. But this, too, varies among the different countries. Perhaps because of its very different culture, Japanese ownership is considered more difficult to work with than others. Some recent problems encountered by Japanese companies that acquired U.S. firms are due to Japanese insistence on more formal management hierarchy and more rigid work rules.

Third, the U.S. government has not uniformly opposed foreign investment but has in fact tacitly encouraged it as a way of improving the American economy. But not when the Fujitsu Company of Japan offered $200 million for an 80 percent share of Fairchild Semiconductor Corporation, a major player in California's Silicon Valley. It was defeated when Commerce Secretary Malcolm Baldrige vehemently opposed it. The fear was that the investment would further the creeping Japanese control of American technology and eventually make the U.S. dependent on the Japanese variety. Is there a relationship between economic security and national security? These were the concerns expressed by the Reagan administration as part of its opposition to the Fujitsu bid. Looking back on that blocked 1987 offer, professional observers believe that the firm government action deterred the Japanese from trying to buy entire high-tech American companies and forced them to limit their efforts to small, minority investments, at least for awhile.

More recently, the Federal government has assumed a more moderate stance on foreign investment, opting for a global economy concept as opposed to protectionism. This is true of both the George Bush and Bill Clinton presidencies. But

President Clinton has also displayed considerable interest in opening up Japanese reciprocal trade to Americans, in expressing much hope over the North American Free Trade Association (NAFTA) and its synergistic effects on U.S. Mexican and Canadian trade, and in freeing the hemisphere of dictatorship. So will the U.S. toughen its stand on foreign investments if, for example, the Japanese incursion into computer chips, automotive and retailing continues to grow? Not very likely.

"It's pretty much of a tradeoff," observes Dr. Carolyn Brancatto, research director of corporate governance for the Conference Board, the non-profit research organization in New York. "Our key concerns are whether we are giving away vital industry linkage, such as in the machine-tool industry," she said in an interview. "But today, we have such a global mentality in the U.S. that we hate to put on any restrictions lest someone restricts us. Our adherence to free-market principles is so ingrained that we feel we have to be role models."

A former Federal government official, she believes that foreign investment has played an important, productive role in the American economy. "It has replaced the falloff in our savings rate, for one thing," she says. "It's provided new jobs and helped many of our local economies. We are now in global markets, with different types of technology. We have to learn them and adapt to others' entrepreneurial drives, use them and add to them. The world, in a word or two, has changed."

Some Interesting Foreign-U.S. Deals

With a successful tender offer that drew a 96 percent response, Cadbury Schweppes P.L.C., the British soft drink-confectionary empire, took over A&W Brands, one of the largest U.S. soft-drink vendors, for $334 million. A&W will be folded into Cadbury's American entity. Up through late 1994, Cadbury was the third-largest soft-drink producer in the world after Coca-Cola and Pepsico and evidently is now playing for a higher position on the international totem pole. Cadbury also boosted its stake in Dr. Pepper/Seven Up Companies, America's third-largest soft-drink maker, to 25.9 percent.

In an international bank deal, the Citizens Financial Group Inc., a unit of the Royal Bank of Scotland P.L.C., paid $122 million in cash to acquire Neworld Bancorp Inc., of Boston, and its Neworld Bank unit. Neworld's 22 banking offices in Massachusetts will be merged into Citizens Bank of Massachusetts, which will now have more than 125 branches in the state, Connecticut and Rhode Island.

Roche Holdings, a major Basel, Switzerland pharmaceuticals maker, paid $5.3 billion in a tender offer for the Syntex Corporation, Palo Alto, California, successfully completing one of the largest cross-border transactions in years. The offer was briefly extended for the completion of an investigation by the U.S. Federal Trade Commission and then resumed after the FTC gave its blessing. Roche agreed to divest some of Syntex's medical diagnostic assets in the U.S.

The Swiss Bank Corporation, intent on expanding its investment banking in the U.S., paid $750 million in stock for Brinson Partners Inc., a Chicago investment management firm. The Zurich-based Swiss Bank in 1992 had acquired O'Connor & Associates, an American futures trading firm. Brinson, formerly the First Chicago Investment Advisors, a unit of First Chicago Corporation, was sold to the unit's managers in 1989 for $85 million and a remaining 10 percent stake. In announcing the deal in August 1994, Swiss Bank said that it was eager to expand its asset management business in the U.S., which it called the world's biggest and fastest-growing market in that field.

And, in an unusual case of two foreign nationals fighting over an American company, Lucas Industries of Slihull, England, paid $87 million to acquire Lake Center Industries, a subsidiary of Guy F. Atkinson Company, topping an $80 million bid by Valeo S.A., of France.

An American Brands unit, the Whyte & Mackay Group, offered to pay $258.1 million for a 45.3 percent stake to obtain full control of the last, independent Scotch whisky distillers, Invergordon Distillers Group P.L.C. of Edinburgh. Earlier, Whyte & Mackay had obtained more Invergordon shares from London investment funds to give it 54.7 percent of the Scotch distilling company. The Old Greenwich, Connecticut-based American Brands is the maker of Jim Beam bourbon, Gilbey's gin and vodka, and has diversified holdings in tobacco, insurance and leisure equipment. Invergordon produces whisky, gin, vodka, and liqueur.

Furthering its continuing European expansion, the Exide Corporation, the Bloomfield Hills Company which is one of the leading car-battery makers, said that it will buy Compagnie Europeene d'Accumulateurs S.A., a unit of Fiat S.p.A., for $535 million. The European company, based in France, Italy and Germany, is an auto battery producer with sales of about $700 million. The new acquisition represented the fourth in Europe in 1994 for Exide, the maker of such battery brands as Exide, Willard and Prestolite.

GE Capital Corporation, the huge financial arm of the General Electric Company, moved to expand more internationally with a $387.5 million purchase of Finax Group, a unit of the Wasa Group of Sweden. The purchase price is made up of $125 million in cash and $262.5 million in assumed debt. Finax is composed of a consumer finance company in Norway and four Swedish companies that provide unsecured personal loans and credit cards to 400,000 customers.

The world's largest funeral home company, the Dallas, Texas-based Service Corporation International, bid to become even bigger with a $152 million offer for the Great Southern Group P.L.C., Great Britain's third-largest funeral home business. A family trust that controlled Great Southern balked at Service Corporation's earlier bid, compelling the Americans to offer 14 percent more which was accepted.

In another electronics acquisition, Pactel Corporation, which is owned by the Pacific Telesis Group, completed a $153 million purchase of a 51 percent interest in Nordictel Holdings, a Swedish cellular phone company. The Nordictel's product is named Europolitan. The Swedish company is owned by four other partners, including the automobile producer Volvo A.B.

The Foreign Takeover Style—Rough and Tumble, Like Ours

When Adrian Sada Gonzalez touched off Mexico's first, hostile bid for an American company in 1989, those in the merger-acquisition business on both sides of the border knew that international diplomacy had undergone a wrenching experience. Mr. Sada, who later headed a much larger Mexican financial company, wasn't reluctant for his Grupo Vitro SA, a glass-container company, to pay $265 million for the Anchor Glass Container Corporation of Tampa, Florida. The American company wasn't so eager. But the then 49-year old Mr. Sada was willing to wait and tough out his bid and eventually won his quarry.

His persistence represented only one instance in which foreign businesspeople and financiers demonstrated that they would happily take off the gloves and barehandedly take over coy, uncertain or downright unwilling businesses.

In Canada in 1994, Edward S. Rogers, a tough, 60-year old entrepreneur and the founder of Rogers Communications Inc., Canada's biggest cable company, was so eager to buy the Maclean Hunter Ltd., the country's largest publishing entity, that he secretly decided that the transaction would virtually be worth any amount of money it would take. Maclean Hunter, publisher of Maclean's, the national newsmagazine, was definitely for sale and "in play." But Ronald W. Osborne, its chairman, didn't want to surrender his company cheaply.

For five weeks, the two CEO's huffed and puffed. The Maclean Hunter stock kept fairly steady at $17 a share, hewing to the level that Rogers had bid. Finally, after the two decided to escape from the investor and media spotlight and hold some secret sessions, Rogers sweetened his offer and Osborne gave in. "Seventeen dollars a share was not adequate," Osborne said, flatly. "Seventeen-fifty *is* adequate." On that bit of bargaining was created Canada's largest communications empire.

But the most dramatic contretemps was occurring in England. In 1988, Nestle, the Swiss chocolate company, launched a hostile offer for Rowntree, a venerable candymaker beloved by the British. The Brits were outraged at this offensive against a national taste icon. Members of Parliament rose to lambaste the government for not stamping out the foreign incursion. Civic groups departed from Rowntree's home town of York to Switzerland in an effort to change Nestle's mind. Local meetings were held in York to rail against the foreign takeover.

The situation became a vicious triangle when the Jacob Suchard AG, another prominent Swiss chocolate maker, entered the fray with a $3.9 billion offer for Rowntree. Besieged on two sides, Nestle nonetheless stood fast, offered $4.25 billion and captured Rowntree. About the only ones who enjoyed the contest were the British newspaper headline writers, whose creative buds were aroused to produce such unworthy puns as "the bar wars."

The Nestle-Rowntree-Suchard go-round was not the only one at the time. The British construction firm Beazer was also pushing a hostile bid for the American Koppers Company, the Pittsburgh, Pennsylvania maker of construction materials. Since Shearson Lehman Hutton, a subsidiary of the American Express Company, was partly financing Beazer's move, the American "defection" brought some heat of its own. Many Pittsburghers were cutting up their American Express credit cards to show their protest against the foreign invasion.

A few months later, Goodman Fielder Wattie of Australia staged an attempt to take over Rank Hovis McDougall, the big British food complex. This, too, created considerable public debate and acid dialogues in Parliament.

Obviously, with invaders from Switzerland and Australia storming their walls at a time when British industrialists were buying such American landmark companies as Koppers, Brooks Brothers and Macmillan Publishing, things were getting sticky for the British. They could hardly protest too much for being criticized themselves.

Obviously, too, the suave Continental manner of doing business had changed. It continued to produce one donnybrook after another in both the United Kingdom and Europe. One was an international brouhaha in gold mining when the Consolidated Gold Fields, a British company with mines in South Africa, was attacked by the South African Anglo American Corporation with a takeover bid of $4.9 billion. After bitter exchanges, charges and countercharges, the bidder got its way. Another war that seemed never to end was the controversial acquisition by an Egyptian investor group headed by the Fayyed brothers of the fabled Harrod's department store in London which led to a host of eruptions including nascent nationalism on the part of the British, charges and counter-charges and severe questions about the ability of non-merchants—foreigners at that—to operate Britain's most treasured department store. Caught in the middle was the British Mergers and Monopolies Commission which wavered and then ruled in favor of the Egyptians. But it didn't much calm the dissension. It continues to simmer to this day.

Then there was the Belgian bombshell when an Italian banker, Carlo de Benedetti, generated a hostile offer for Belgium's biggest company, the Societe Generale de Belgique. Belgians were much aroused at this economic imperialism. But then the Belgian stock market boomed, introducing that normally dignified country into the trading frenzy that the U.S. and Japanese stock markets know so well.

What did the new brass-knuckles tendency show to British and Continental business? Foremost, the reality that Americans had known for years—that no business or industry is sacrosanct in terms of takeover. Money, personal drive and willing partners eager to profit from a merger or acquisition form a potent combination when the smell of weakness, indolence or rank opportunity rises to the surface. Moreover, they learned that short of a harsh, governmental crackdown on rampant domestic takeovers or foreign incursion, there is little that can be done to thwart a hostile, well-financed bidder. In the U.S., some have been halted by the defensive armament that includes "poison pills," a buying sweep of a company's own stock or the enactment of state curbs. But the first two are expensive and controversial while the third becomes a political football that is hard to control.

But what of Japan, where "nottori," the term denoting hijacking, was long used to denigrate business takeovers?

That term isn't much used anymore because M&As in Japan have grown rapidly from almost a standing start a decade ago. Because the Japanese companies needed to expand internationally since the domestic turf was already carefully staked out, they began buying foreign companies, including many in the U.S., in an industry range that included chemicals, hotels, tires and retailing. The strength of the yen, the country's basic currency, was and is the main determinant that prompts or slows such takeovers. Yet the Japanese are such believers in the long-term aspect as opposed to temporal problems that even in the more turbulent times for the yen, their merger-acquisition appetite wasn't much affected. They were simply willing to pay more.

Among their larger U.S. acquisitions were a $535 million deal for Reichhold Chemicals Inc.; Aoki Hotels' $1.3 billion purchase of the Westin Hotels chain; Bridgestone's $2.6 billion deal for Firestone Tire & Rubber Company; and Dainippon Ink & Chemicals' $550 million takeover of the graphic arts unit of the Sun Chemical Company. The Bridgestone-Firestone transaction for $2.6 billion and the Sony $2 billion buyout of CBS Records were the two largest Japanese-U.S. transactions until 1990 when they were far exceeded by the $6.1 billion purchase of MCA Inc., the entertainment and movie production company, by the Matsushita Electrical Industrial Company.

As in the case with other foreign buyers of U.S. properties, American investment bankers acted as starters or middlemen. First Boston Corporation, Goldman Sachs and Morgan Stanley opened branches in Japan and rapidly expanded them. But the Japanese, despite their different ways of doing business, are quick learners. Not only did their banks open offices in the U.S. and begin employing M&A specialists but they also started buying into some of the best-known merger-and-acquisition companies in the U.S. Perhaps the best example is Nomura Securities Company's $100 million investment in Wasserstein, Perella & Company. It was a classic move, the biggest Japanese securities house buying a major stake in one of the most active, American M&A companies. Obvious target: the U.S.

This conclusion isn't hard to come by. Thus far, while the Japanese are becoming more and more aggressive in their foreign acquisitions, that is hardly the case in Japan. Tradition is hard to break. Many Japanese companies still preserve a diplomatic dignity toward one another. Their senior managements, too, are loath to give up a company or parts of it which have been owned for long decades by the same families or have been in business for a long time. Then there's the high price that Japanese domestic consolidations require, a compound of such things as higher price/earnings multiples, the sky-high cost of real-estate and the fixed costs generated by lifetime employment, usually from 50 percent to 75 percent more than U.S. acquisitions would cost Japanese companies.

How Compatible Are Japanese and American Executives?

What happens when the culture (call it business credo) gap festers and eventually erupts into a serious dissension between the Japanese owners and the top management of the American company that they bought?

That happened between Matsushita and MCA in 1994, four years after this significant acquisition took place. It began when Lew Wasserman, MCA's chairman, and Sidney Sheinberg, president, asked Matsushita for more autonomy for MCA which they had continued to manage under employment contracts. They had become increasingly frustrated because they weren't being allowed to acquire companies that would allow them to build a much more diversified entertainment conglomerate. They insisted that they had to compete with the more muscular companies such as Time Warner and Viacom-Paramount Communications, both of which had combined their individual facilities into powerful organizations through mergers. But the Japanese, particularly Masaharu Matsushita, the company chairman, refused to be pushed into concessions that might prove costly and unproductive. Even the threat by Wasserman and Sheinberg that they would terminate their contracts did not seem to sway the parent company.

The situation came to a boil on the night of Tuesday, October 18, when the two sides confronted one another in a four-hour meeting at San Francisco's Mark Hopkins Hotel. The heated discussion only made things worse. No reporters were allowed in, of course. But it doesn't take much imagination to envision the stirring anger of the two grand old men, 82-year old Masaharu Matsushita and 81-year old Lew Wasserman as they glared at each other, their associates seated uncomfortably around them, and tried to bridge the many centuries and many miles that separated their cultures.

It was obvious that Matsushita's management respected the two Americans for what they knew and for their stewardship of the U.S. subsidiary. Starting as a leading talent agency and evolving over the 52 years of Wasserman's tenure into one of the leading U.S. film and television producers,MCA had just completed a very rewarding 1993. Sales were estimated at about $4 billion a year and operating profit at about $400 million. As the unhappy participants filed out after stiff bows between the two parties, the strong possibility lingered that Matsushita just might decide to sell MCA to rid itself of a troublesome subsidiary that was more petulant than it was worth to a company with $60 billion sales.

Would Wasserman-Sheinberg make a pitch for the company? It was not mentioned at the meeting but often was in the days and weeks afterward along with the names of other possible bidders. MCA, after all, was a great, shining bauble.

Matsushita and MCA's unhappiness with each other might have appeared intractible. But it's quite possible that it isn't so much over drastically different business philosophies as over a rift in manners or personality differences or both. The culture gap between the two nations is still wide despite all the contact they have had with each other since World War II ended a half-century ago.

But in April 1995, Matsushita threw in the sponge. It agreed to sell 80 percent of MCA for $5.7 billion to the Seagram Company.

The experience of Sally Frame-Kazak, the president of the Ann Taylor specialty stores, may shed some light on the problem of Japanese-American relations. A much-respected fashion merchant, Ms. Frame-Kazak was president in the early 1980s of Talbots, a retail chain featuring New England classic women's clothes, when it was purchased by the Jusco Company, a major Japanese retail company. She left for another post after only three months with the foreign owners, but today recalls her contacts with the Japanese in general and with Masaharu Isogai, the chairman of Jusco, in particular.

"When I first started travelling to Japan," she said in an interview, "I didn't know what was considered polite and what wasn't. I was uncomfortable at first. I was tall, many Japanese men were short and the bowing process could be awkward. But I got over that. The big problem for me was understanding the manners. No one held a door open for you whereas in New York they at least give it a tap for you. In fact, in Japan, people try getting on an elevator before they let others get out. Yet, they are polite in their own way. They bow when you meet them, they are solicitous, they try hard not to embarrass you. But," she added, "it's hard to balance out those manners."

But it was in working with Isogai that the confusion disappeared.

When Isogai and his team came to Talbots' offices and spent time there, "It was apparent that the Japanese were cognizant of our differences, were sensitive to them and were anxious to make a smooth transition. Everyone tried hard, too, to make that happen," said Ms. Frame-Kazak. As head of the American company, she was particularly sensitive to the fact that she was a new employee, a woman at that and still not quite certain of how to behave toward the Japanese.

"But when Mr. Isogai and I visited the Talbots' stores together, everything fell into place," she said. "We were able to communicate as merchants. There is a common language in business, regardless of nationality. Businessmen and business women share the same values, even though culturally they can be very different. Even though their manners are different and their organizational situation is different. But the reality is that when I went into a store with Mr. Isogai, I had more rapport with him as a merchant than I had later with the chairman of a diversified American company."

In other words, when it comes to business, outward differences do not mean very much. What counts instead are solid operating principles. Maybe eventually that will be the bridge to solve some pervading problems between the two giant economies.

Sony Bites the Bullet

Outward differences or not, Sony, the huge Japanese electronics company which in 1989 had acquired Columbia Pictures and

Tristar Pictures, finally acknowledged after months of optimistic disclaimers that those two American subsidiaries were having serious problems.

So serious, said Sony in its bombshell announcement on November 18, 1994 that it was taking a massive $3.2 billion loss in the value of those two Hollywood movie studios. Due to the studios' poor box office results, executive departures and ever-rising costs, Sony said that it could never hope to recover its investment. The loss included a $2.7 billion loss in value and $510 million in further losses in three months from July 1 to September 30. The latter was the result of cancellations of movies in development, the settlement of litigation and payment of large sums to departing executives. Only if it were willing to plow yet more money into the studios could Sony hope to push them into the black.

It was one of the largest quarterly losses ever suffered by a major Japanese company and a source of considerable embarrassment to Sony, long considered one of the best-managed Japanese businesses. The timing of the dramatic announcement came ironically only a few days after the announcement that the giant Mitsubishi Estate Company might have to default on the mortgage of Rockefeller Center, one of New York City's largest office-and-entertainment complexes, which it had bought a few years before. The Sony, Mitsubishi and Matsushita problems with MCA were immediately seen as symptoms of a difficult Japanese economy. But once the dust began settling, another level of analysis set in in which the inability of Japanese to manage their American acquisitions was seen as the core problem. For Sony, one was with the executives it hired shortly after it bought the studios. Two successful film producers, Jon Peters and Peter Guber, were brought in to run them. But Sony found itself in a difficult position on their remuneration because legal disputes arose over the duo's contracts with rival producing companies. So Sony would up paying a staggering $700 million to hire them.

The second problem apparently was the movies that Sony approved for production. Most proved to be box-office disasters, including "The Last Action Hero," "Lost in Yonkers," "I'll Do Anything" and "Mary Shelley's Frankenstein."

All that was further complicated by the fact that Jon Peters left shortly after being hired, as did Peter Guber, only a few weeks before Sony's surprising announcement. Whether they realized that sorry state of the studios and decided to leave them in other hands or left for other reasons was not clear. But what was clear was that the Columbia and Tristar studios rested at the bottom of the heap among movie companies in share of market.

The decision by Sony to take its lumps on the studios stemmed from "a strategic analysis," said Michael P. Schulhof, president of Sony Corporation of America. No further details were volunteered as to the strategy except that costs would be tightened and efforts would be made to reestablish the studios' former market share. But Schulhof added, "Sony's enthusiasm and commitment to its motion picture, television and video businesses are undiminished."

Should We Worry About the Foreign Incursion?

As James B. Lee of the Chase Manhattan Corporation noted in the previous chapter, foreign buyout of American companies will continue as long as the U.S. dollar remains cheap relative to other currencies. As the European nations rebound from their recession, they will grow stronger and cast an even more acquisitive eye toward the U.S. The same goes for Japan, Lee says.

But, there's nothing more effective than a sensitive awareness to likely events. The moral: stay alert and tuned.

part three

The People Who Make It
Happen

chapter 9

Wall Street's New, Newer, Newest Breeds

Wall Street, never quite the same since the "Black Monday" in October 1987 when business mergers virtually came to a dead stop, has witnessed a shuffling of faces and bodies that defies previous standards, hiring practices and clubby mores.

Gone are the senior types with button-down shirts, Brooks Brothers' natural suits and the occasional far-off expressions signifying a withheld desire for golfing greens and country-club terraces. Where before it used to be "the importance of being earnest," now it's the earnestness of being important. That means a steadfast work ethic demonstrated by long hours with the laptops in the office or on the road, a ceaseless desire to help clients solve their corporate and even personal problems, and especially the capacity to help them improve their price/earnings multiples. Mergers, acquisitions, divestitures and the like are often a way of doing all this.

If you think those changes denote a younger, better educated and more diverse, ethnic mix, then you've got it just about right.

Stephen A. Schwarzman, 47 years old, is president and chief executive officer of The Blackstone Group, a medium-sized "boutique" New York investment banking house prominent in merger-and-acquisition activity. In 1985, with Peter G. Peterson, former U.S. Secretary of Commerce under President Richard Nixon, Schwarzman started Blackstone. Later, they were joined by David A. Stockman, who had been national budget director under President Ronald Reagan. One of the busiest and most successful M&A men, Schwarzman, in my view, is characteristic of the new Wall Street M&A practitioners. He is a fast-talking, innovative type who commands plenty of respect.

Steven Rattner, general partner at Lazard Freres & Company, is 42 years old and is a former economics reporter of the *New York Times* with whom I worked. Concentrating on media deals at Lazard, Steve worked on the merger of Viacom and Paramount Communications. Though he is only five years younger than Schwarzman, I see him as the newer type of M&A expert on Wall Street, partly because he comes from another field of endeavor but has found the buying and selling of companies so personally challenging.

The "baby" of the three, Henry D. Jackson, a principal of the Peter J. Solomon Company, is only 31 at this writing but is, I think, aging fast. He was involved in the Federated takeover of Macy's among other retailing mergers, a process that will quickly mature anyone. He's the newest of the lot, a self-disciplined, hyperenergetic man with his feet solidly planted on the ground. His constant smile of anticipation imparts the idea that everything is open to him and it probably is.

The Wisdom of Solomon

Before I get into the prolonged discussions I recently had with all three, I want to comment briefly about Peter J. Solomon, Henry Jackson's boss, whom I have known for about 25 years and not just as the merger-acquisition expert that he has been during most of that time. Now 54, Peter is also a former Deputy Mayor of New York City for economic development and has also worked for the Federal government in Washington in several high posts.

Peter has a salty, incisive way of speaking and has a rare understanding of corporate behavior so that he has no trouble breaking through the protective walls chief executives erect around themselves. In the late 1980s, he invented the "bridge loan" by which investment bankers advance the financing a takeover or target company needs to carry on until full bank financing is arranged. It was a practice that other investment bankers soon picked up. But he never got the credit for it that he deserved. His attitude is "fine if you know it, okay if you don't."

In some random comments on the merger scene, the feisty Solomon, puffing deeply on his cigar, observed, "Most commentators talk about Wall Street firms chasing after clients, especially in restructuring or merger actions to build up ongoing relationships. But in the early 1970s, these relationships crumbled because there was a batch of corporate chief financial officers who started playing one investment banker against another. This created consternation on the street, changes in fees and lots of bruised feelings. A lot of people still haven't forgotten it. In hostile deals, the attacker usually overpays. He or she usually doesn't know or have sufficient knowledge of the internal situation. Like the fact that it is hard to promptly replace management even when you know in advance that it must be replaced. Acquisitions per se are a pot-luck situation, especially if they result in uprooting a founder or longtime CEO. The company isn't the same after that. In fact, the record on acquisitions is tremendously uneven. The ones doing LBOs have done a little better. Especially when they allow the operators to stay in place, because that gives the company a chance to survive after the deal."

The Eagerness of Schwarzman

It's not boastful; it's factual when Stephen A. Schwarzman, the president and chief executive officer of the Blackstone Group, says, "We democratized Wall Street."

At first when I arrived at Blackstone's Manhattan offices, the evidently harassed Schwarzman was not anxious to see me. He was up to his ears, was very curt, but then as we talked he opened up, warming to his subject. The problem was that it was disruptive to philosophize or opine in the mid-afternoon of a very busy day. But he had a lot to say.

What is stirring the nation's ongoing merger trend is "an immutable, cyclical phenomenon" which he has noticed in his 22 years in the field. When the economy is decreasing or decelerating, merger activity goes down, he said. This is because the CEOs and boards of directors who make decisions to buy companies tend not to want to risk their own financial situation when they can't trust their own company's financial results, let alone trust someone else's. So merger activity decelerates and when the bottom of a recession is reached, says Schwarzman, there is a little bit of activity, but not much, because people aren't very optimistic. When the economy turns up, usually after a six-to-nine-month lag, merger activity starts up again.

What is noteworthy in this cyclical recovery, Schwarzman said, is that many of the deals are basically strategic ones done by corporate buyers with the goals of lowering costs or increasing revenues in the area in which they already operate. "That's facilitated by the fact that stock prices are high and money is cheap," he said. "And stocks can be used to buy companies outright or to 'finance the deals out' after purchase on a very favorable basis so you have all the financial instruments available to facilitate mergers."

The strategic concept, he said, is very pervasive in recent mergers. GE trying to buy Kemper fits perfectly where GE is trying to go strategically. Kemper's large real-estate component fits right into GE Capital. The Kemper money management business fits in with what GE Capital wants to do. (Conseco outbid GE for Kemper but withdrew its offer.) "Federated going after Macy's is just another classic example. A lot of the telecommunications mergers where people are basically protecting market share and hedging themselves against technical obsolescence is a classic and strategic business combination which will continue for the next several years. So at the moment the present marketplace doesn't value conglomerates particularly because there's not much of a reason to assemble that type of package. With prices high, if you can buy something with business synergy your stock will be better because your earnings will be better."

Future mergers? "I don't see the return of the conglomerates," Schwarzman said. "There ought to be continued activity in banking. It's the economic law of the jungle to squeeze out weaker competitors in that area as the larger ones spread their costs over a bigger base. There should be continued activity in telecommunications. You'll have a booming business in the health-care merger market caused at the start by the U.S. government's proposals which are being reacted to by both the Congress and the customers, as well as the health-care industry itself. The cat is now permanently out of the bag in terms of cost-containment which is going to change the face of the health-care industry as we know it in a fundamental way."

Invited to talk about Blackstone, he said, "We have worked with some of the biggest companies in the world," he said, "including Pepsico, Sony and Mitsubishi, Nestle, and others. Business flows through a variety of ways. We also have a capital pool of about $1.3 billion where we buy companies ourselves which is actually quite helpful in figuring out where markets are. Our advisory side has some ideas and our principal side has some ideas. Another thing we do that gets us involved in the merger business is our restructuring activity. We have a group, for example, which has been working with Macy's to develop a restructuring plan and will become involved in merger negotiations when that happens. And typically in a lot of our restructuring activity, there is an M&A component because one of the alternatives that typically faces a group of creditors or equity holders is selling the business outright to a third party as opposed to just restructuring. So we have three different areas of the business that get involved with M&A activity."

Schwarzman, a graduate of Yale majoring in psychology with an MBA from Harvard Graduate School of Business Administration, is a sort of quiet legend on Wall Street. After beginning his career in 1972 at Lehman Brothers, he was elected a managing director in 1978 at the age of 31. One of the period's biggest takeovers was brewing—the Beatrice Foods acquisition of Tropicana. It was a Lehman Brothers deal. Despite his youth and lack of experience, Steve emerged as the senior person on the account and was responsible for cementing the transaction. "It was very exciting, certainly a high-impact event for me," he recalled. "Mainly, it was because the deal was so large, even though later on there were bigger deals that I worked on. I worked very long hours at Lehman for years and I loved it."

His entry into Lehman at the onset of the 1970s was one of the Wall Street appointments that marked the arrival of a new group of fledgling investment bankers specializing in the then still new area of M&A's. They were all well educated, mostly Ivy League and MBA's and in their early 30s. They replaced the old, gentleman crowd who had grown up selling stocks, bonds and doing occasional mergers, knowing and at home in a quieter and less complex world of finance. So the new men fanned out throughout Wall Street—Schwarzman at Lehman, Bruce Wasserstein and Joseph Perella at First Boston, Tomilson Hill at Shearson—and brought a new, younger, more brash temperament into the business of buying and selling companies.

"The merger business is essentially a violent game," Schwarzman said. "You either win or you lose and that's it. There's a very conflict-oriented underpinning to it. It's not a contest for people who just want to be comfortable. The older guys were beginning to feel alien to the first signs of violent confrontation and were, I think, glad to get out of it. Why get involved with messy conflicts? But for the younger guys, the M&A business was ripe for us to make our mark. My class of Harvard MBA's was the first MBA class that Lehman Brothers hired. That was back in 1972. I think you can call it the 'democratization of Wall Street,'" Steve said. "We weren't socially elegant or claiming a distinguished lineage but we were certainly eager. And we did make our mark."

As Blackstone's president and chief executive officer, Schwarzman did make his mark in spearheading and financing a dozen mergers with a range in value from $125 million to $2.6 billion. In a 1993 deal, Blackstone Capital Partners, Blackstone's investment fund, provided $375 million to seal a $1.6 billion transaction to acquire Univa Ltd., one of Canada's biggest supermarket operators. The $11-a-share offer, made in conjunction with Unigesco, Univa's largest shareholder, was 45 percent higher than Univa's public market price over the 20 days prior to the February 9, 1993 offer. Despite nationalistic grumbling by some Canadians, the offer was snapped up.

A smaller U.S. deal also involved Blackstone Capital Partners. In February 1993, Blackstone's Hospitality Franchise Systems Inc. paid $125 million for Super 8 Motels Inc., which owned 950 budget-priced motels in the U.S. Setting up investment pools like Blackstone Capital Partners, with private investors, has been one of the characteristic innovations of the new crowd. It has turned many a buyout from being just a gleam in someone's eye into becoming an actual event.

Although Blackstone isn't in the same major league with, say, a Merrill Lynch, it has become a formidable, if smaller contender among the Wall Street bankers and M&A players. Peter Peterson's important corporate contacts made when he was chairman-CEO of Lehman Brothers, president and CEO of Bell & Howell and later in the cabinet, David Stockman's experience in the White House top hierarchy, and Steven Schwarzman's own Wall Street experience have combined to give Blackstone a very impressive imprimatur.

The Earnestness of Rattner

Like many another business and financial writer, I have sometimes wondered how a business journalist might fare in business, not just as a public-relations man or woman because there are lots of them who are ex-reporters. I mean actually in business, on the profit-making firing-line. My point is that we as reporters spout off, telling CEOs what to do, where to get off and in being (if we are any good at all) a general pain in the rear. But how would we do in their place? Up until I met Steven Rattner of Lazard Freres & Company, I personally knew of only two who had successfully made the switch. One was George Mooney, a *New York Times* financial writer, who became New York State's Superintendent of Banking. The other is Carl Spielvogel, who was an advertising columnist for the *Times,* and later became one of the biggest men in the advertising business.

Steve Rattner is a soft-spoken, blondish, boyish-looking fellow, who comes across as a sort of milder Robert Redford. But he has been an absolute "wow" on Wall Street without seeking a lot of fanfare because it has naturally flowed to him in major-media quotes and in interviews on television, especially because of deals he's been in. Soft-spoken or not, Steve got Lazard into the $12.6 billion merger between AT&T and McCaw Cellular Communications. He also devised the financing by which McCaw obtained control of Lin Broadcasting by outbidding BellSouth Corporation.

Remember what I said about the new breed's "earnestness"? Steve exudes it. In November 1993, the *Wall Street Journal* in a prominent piece speculated that Steve Rattner "has emerged as the firm's strongest banker after Mr. (Felix) Rohatyn," Lazard's chairman who helped pioneer the conglomerate trend and who in the 1970s saved New York City from bankruptcy, and that Steve might be Rohatyn's successor. The newspaper noted that "the investment banking fees generated by Mr. Rattner rank second only to those brought in by Mr. Rohatyn and are more than twice that of the firm's next most productive banker." ·

Of course, that's speculation and there's plenty of air between possible and real. But certainly one gets no whiff of an upward push or pomposity when visiting Rattner in his rather plain, crowded office in Rockefeller Plaza in Manhattan. In shirt-sleeves, with a bemused expression and making a determined search for some elusive papers to answer a question or two, he would never give you any impression that he was a guy who reportedly earned $5 million in 1993, has three homes and flies his own, eight-seat Cessna airplane.

"There's an enormous upheaval in media stimulated by regulatory activity and new technology," Rattner says in his matter-of-fact way, "and it's created some big takeover deals. Also, in health-care, the M&A activity is growing fueled by a general move to contain margins. I don't know if you can call it all a boom yet but it's certainly getting there. And it's keeping me busy."

Rattner was born in Great Neck, New York. He attended Brown University, graduating in 1974, earning honors in economics and winning a fellowship. In 1973, he joined the *New York Times*, first as assistant to James Reston, the newspaper's executive editor, and later columnist, and then as a correspondent in New York, Washington, and London. "It was when I was in London," he told me, "that I decided to make the change. I wanted to see what life was like on the other side of the fence from journalism. I was 30 years old. It seemed like a worthwhile experiment at the time. It was hard leaving the *Times* but I figured I could always go back to journalism. In two years, I would know if I liked the change."

He started on Wall Street in 1982 at Lehman Brothers where in 18 months he received a grounding in M&As. When the firm was sold to Shearson, Steve left to join Morgan Stanley, where he founded a communications group which engaged in both mergers and financing during the five years he was there. The M&As he assisted in totaled more than $15 billion in value and he also helped raise more than $4 billion in capital. "After Morgan Stanley," Rattner said, "I decided to go with a smaller, private firm, Lazard Freres, where the opportunities would be greater because I was needed more there than at Morgan." Lazard was one-tenth the size, employing only about 800 against Morgan Stanley's approximate 8,000.

"What I had going for me everywhere I went," he said, "was that I was young and I could always start over again. At Lehman, they could try me out cheaply but everywhere else they would have to pay me more so that it was more of a risk both for me and for them. One thing I gradually learned wherever I went. I decided that I was better at finance than at journalism. I felt that finance came naturally to me. It was very interesting and challenging and it was rewarding from an earnings standpoint."

Yet he knew as he worked in the finance side of the business that there were "a lot of people who didn't do it for the money. These were mostly older people who got their kicks from the excitement that is at the heart of the money business. Besides," added Steve, "on any given project, you have to be objective about it to be successful. The money you make from it is secondary."

But it all takes patience and resilience, he added. "Of all the projects you get under way, you're successful only in a minority of them."

How important are the personalities of the principal players? "That depends on both the deal and the personalities," he replied. "In some deals, chemistry doesn't matter much but it varies. In others, where top teamwork is especially vital and senior executives know they'll have to work closely together, it's of enormous importance. But if it's a case where the CEO of the target company plans to retire when the deal is consummated, the personality of the acquiring company's CEO doesn't matter."

Is there something unique in every deal? "I learn something from every deal because there's always something different in each one," Steve said. "But, frankly, I learn more from my mistakes, especially how I can avoid making the same ones again."

Evidently, he hasn't made very many in the five years he has been at Lazard Freres. He's part of senior management now as co-head of investment banking as well as general partner. As at Morgan Stanley, he founded a communications group at Lazard, now consisting of seven professionals. In his tenure, Rattner has started or completed more than $70 billion in media transactions.

What's the M&A outlook? "The trend will grow in intensity through 1995 and beyond, short-term. But inevitably, other sectors of the economy will come into greater play as transactions," he says. But in the remaining years of the 1990s, he said, he wasn't certain that each year would show an upward trend from the year before. "It will probably be very cyclical, up and down."

Despite his conviction that he's a better banker than journalist, Steve still writes occasional pieces for the *New York Times*, the *Wall Street Journal* and *Newsweek*. It seems that you can take the guy out of the newsroom but you can't make him turn off the word processor.

So, perhaps the final point about Rattner is—what makes a former journalist so good at buying and selling companies and at raising capital? I like to think it's the analytical skills he developed as a reporter. But more likely, he's just plain good at what he does—and why can't it be that simple?

The Entrepreneurship of Jackson

When I interviewed Henry D. Jackson of the Peter J. Solomon Company, I found him so articulate and given to interesting detail that I decided to let him tell his story in his own words.

"I was born in New York—actually in New York University Hospital, to be precise—and we lived in Riverdale, moved to Westchester County and then to Roslyn, Long Island when I was 12. You mention that I look so young. The reason is that I am young, 31. I was born in 1964. I went to the University of Pennsylvania and the Wharton School where they had a dual degree program. I studied finance and international relations and graduated in 1986.

"At Wharton, I graduated near the top of my class and I was recruited by a number of Wall Street firms. Wharton has a wonderful program and in the Eighties it was a hot breeding ground for the investment banks. They solicited us very aggressively. Goldman Sachs, First Boston, Morgan Stanley, Drexel, the big, prestigious firms. They sent out limousines to take us to the best restaurants to convince us to go to work for them. It was an unbelievable time. Twenty-one-year-old kids being chauffeured around in limousines in Philadelphia to the most expensive restaurants, places where we had never gone in four years in school. And being wined and dined. Making the decision later was as much a personality fit as the reputation of the company. During those interviews, you got different vibes about them. Goldman Sachs struck me as very haughty. I liked Morgan Stanley. When I got right down to it, the people I met at First Boston seemed very, very bright. They seemed very capable. The firm was doing extremely well at that time; Morgan was doing less well.

"First Boston was just a tremendous personality fit; I don't know how else to describe it. I started as an analyst in their famous analyst program which was supposed to be a two-year program after which they sent you back to business school. But since I had already been to business school, the company said I didn't have to go. Also, because I chose to enter an industry group—it was retailing and I was the first one in it—rather than a securities group, they wanted me to stay on because I knew a lot about the retail business by then. I originally wanted the broader exposure that an industry group could give me because I had always been entrepreneurial.

"I was an entrepreneur from the time I was 16. My first business—it sounds bizarre today—was at Roslyn High School. I coordinated a party for 1,500 people at a night-club called Xenon. It was a hot disco in the early 1970s and 1980s. I dug up $10,000 which was all I could put together from my own resources and friends, and paid it to the club in advance. We rented the club for that night, took over the door and gave them a guarantee for the bar. We brought in 1,500 people at $15 a head and that gave us $22,500. And we got our $5,000 back on the bar, as well. So that was $27,500 gross, less the $10,000 which was $5,000 for the bar and $5,000 at the door. So we made about $17,000. I wasn't even old enough to drive yet. We used a car service back and forth from the city. It was all money collected from the people at the door. There were bags of cash on the floor at 4 in the morning, staring at us. It was fun. But walking out of the door afterward with the $27,000—remember we had already paid the $10,000 advance—I remember feeling very concerned about it. We got into the limousine very quickly.

"And then we incorporated ourselves. I continued to do more of those, about four or five more. I started syndicating these things in which I would set up the evening, have the invitations printed and then I would bring in partners who would go out and sell it. Where did I get the idea in the first place? I really don't know except that I was dating the daughter of Xenon's owner and I guess it occurred to me that it would be a fun evening and a great way to make some money.

"At college, I also got involved in a business. I got into costume jewelry and we sold a lot to the New York stores. At Wharton, I did something, too. I hired an artist from the school newspaper and we created a caricature of Ben Franklin, which became our trademark. We printed up some tee shirts using different variations of that caricature. One was Ben Franklin standing between two seven-foot basketball players.

"At First Boston, when I started in the new industry group, they asked me to do a retailing study. I did some interviews with analysts and companies and I came back with a big report. I also got involved in corporate finance and visited companies. My first big coup was the Home Depot. They wanted to give First Boston some of their business but there was no one there to talk to in investment banking. We had a great retail analyst, but no one full-time in retailing investment banking. So I went down to Atlanta and saw Bernie Marcus, the chairman and co-founder. He said to me, 'If you can find a way for me to get into the New York market, you'll be my investment banker.'

"It was a nice challenge. A few weeks later on a Saturday afternoon, I was in a Modell store in East Meadow, Long Island, looking to buy a Frisbie. It's an old story. It was a 60,000-70,000 square foot store and you could have thrown the Frisbee across the store without hitting a customer. The parking lot was empty. It was fabulous real estate. Sunday night, I went back into the office and did some research on Modell's. I found they had a lot of stores on Long Island and in New Jersey but they were doing no business. Monday morning, we called Marcus and said, 'Bernie, we have a way for you to get into New York.' A year later, we finally negotiated a deal for him to acquire the Modell stores on Long Island. That's how Home Depot got into the New York market and how First Boston became Home Depot's investment banker and has been ever since.

"So we had some successes. Our group got bigger and grew to 12 people. We did M&A, corporate finance, ESOPs, real estate transactions, LBOs. I was promoted from analyst to associate which was unusual. I was ranked at the top of my group. But one day, a headhunter called me and said, 'Would you like to help start a business with a guy from Lehman?' I said no. I was doing real well at First Boston. Sure, typically, I was working 100 hours a week but they were good to me. I started there out of college at $50,000 and that was an incredible amount of money for a new college graduate. But, I know it sounds silly, it wasn't just the money but the experience I was getting. I was travelling all around the country, making deals, big transactions, and here I was, what, 22 years old and involved in major deals. Was I aware that I was participating in some important economic activity? I don't think so. I and the rest of us were so caught up in the M&A stuff that it seemed like just a normal, business activity. It's hard to appreciate the underlying meaning of what you're doing when you are in the middle of it.

"You ask why I left to join the new company when I had already turned it down? Well, First Boston had gotten into some real problems, with that bridge loan to Campeau and other very bad loans. I didn't leave because of that but because of the chance to start a new company. The first time around, I didn't know that the offer involved Peter Solomon and I had heard a lot about him. But when I found out that it was him, I did some research on him. The main question I had to ask— remember this was 1989 in the days of Ivan Boesky and so on— was he honest? Yes, everyone said, he's honest and he has integrity. He's very well regarded. And so I went with him.

"That was five years ago. And I've been very busy every day since then."

chapter 10

The Big Players

Almost all the big merger players of the late 1990s can be described as tough. That translates into a determined, tunnel-visioned, no-nonsense, ultra-practical, rather flinty temperament.

There are about 20 of them, but I will concentrate on the most interesting dozen. I may be missing one or two of the best but you can decide for yourself.

What constitutes a "big player"? I am taking a broad view of "big," meaning that the activity can involve just one big, recent deal, or a bunch of them, or a series of smaller deals. The common denominator of "big" in this case is the significance of the acquisitions or mergers depending upon their size, prominent public perception and the large sums paid for them. I must confess, however, that given a choice between one "big" and another, I chose the one whose buying and dealing tendencies were colorful, dramatic or suspenseful.

Now the "big" and the "tough" aren't always apparent. In fact, the "tough" is sometimes so hidden that you couldn't possibly know it was part of the person's makeup until sometime later when it bursts forth and surprises you. But some of these big players keep the "tough" under constant vigil and come across as genial, friendly souls. For example, there's Donald Trump. He's the New York real-estate entrepreneur and Atlantic City, New Jersey casino owner who's constantly threatening to buy this or that outside his normal province, gets lots of media play for it but only sometimes does buy the property. It doesn't matter. By dint of startups and acquisitions, he's already one of the most important men in New York and Atlantic City.

But what a technique he has. I called him one evening and he came right to the phone. When I told him who it was, he said, right off, "Say, I'm glad to talk to you. I've often admired your work. You really know what you're doing. Now what did you want to ask me?" That really threw me off my stride. His graciousness was very unusual. I was certain that it was a calculated thing but I still liked it. Newspapermen and women are more than slightly paranoid, certain that no one likes or (more important) respects them. So when someone demonstrates such courtesy, it tends to floor us, at least for a few moments.

Now here's the kicker to this story. Another younger, financial writer on the *New York Times* with whom I was friendly asked me one day if I knew Donald Trump. When I said yes, he said, "What's with him? He's giving me a real hard time. He tells me that I'm inaccurate as hell. I don't know what I'm doing. I don't know what to do about it."

"Do you want me to talk to him?"

"No. I have to do this on my own. I'll work it out somehow."

As far as I know, they came to a sort of accommodation and began getting along somewhat better. But I couldn't help thinking what a different perception of Donald Trump we both had. Donald may not like it much but I have a suspicion that his behavior toward my younger colleague was more typical than his behavior toward me. I saw him again at some business-social event when I introduced my wife to him and he was again most gracious. So go figure. But I still say "tough."

Now for my list of the big players.

The Media Moguls: Murdoch, Turner and Black

Rupert Murdoch. Few people have cut such a swath in international media as he has. He was born in 1931 in Australia and eventually came to dominate 70 percent of that continent's newspapers. He had a personal drive that was hard to put down. Combining a penchant for sensational, tabloid journalism with a sharp talent for promotion, he accumulated by the age of 50 an international media empire, buying one newspaper after another, as well as a 50 percent share of Twentieth Century Fox, the American movie production company, six Metromedia television stations and magazine publishing companies.

Wherever there was a troubled newspaper, magazine or television station rumored to be going on the block, his presence was ubiquitous. No property was too austere, too big, too costly or too shlocky for him to display serious interest. He even purchased a 50 percent stake in a Hungarian tabloid, Reform. In London he eventually controlled the three largest newspapers, the *Sun,* the *News of the World* and the *Times.* In New York he acquired the *New York Post,* the nation's oldest newspaper, the *Village Voice* and *New York* magazine. Editors were hired impulsively and fired quickly if they displeased him. Total loyalty and obedience were what he demanded.

He became a major figure in British television, owning 50 percent of SKY Television, the United Kingdom's first satellite TV service, through his News International which was a wholly-owned subsidiary of the Australian-based News Corporation. In November 1990, he merged SKY Television with its archrival, British Satellite Broadcasting, to form British SKY Broadcasting. By the mid-1990s, every major medium of any sort here and abroad knew that Murdoch's shadow might fall upon them and change their leisurely ways forever.

Robert Edward Turner 3rd, known as "Ted." A truly authentic, heroic, American prototype, Ted Turner could be viewed as our answer to the Australian Murdoch. He was born in Cincinnati in 1938 and attended Brown University. But he left school in 1961 to work for the family's billboard advertising company. When his father committed suicide, Ted took over the business. Over the next quarter-century, he, too, built a media-entertainment empire which includes WTBS, a sports and entertainment cable TV channel; CNN, a much respected cable TV news network and the MGM/UA Entertainment Company. But Turner also had a love of sports, and to make money from something he loved he bought both the Atlanta Braves professional baseball team and the Atlanta Hawks basketball team. In 1977, his yacht won the America's cup.

Unlike Murdoch who comes across as a rather stern, humorless man, Ted Turner has an easy way about him that helps to ease his entrée anywhere. One gathers, too, that he is one of those businessmen who has a conscience about his responsibility. He was the prime promoter of the Goodwill Games, an Olympic-style competition for the physically handicapped, first held in 1986 in Moscow. But I suspect that despite all he has done, nothing gives Ted Turner a more enthusiastic acceptance by the public than the fact that he's married to Jane Fonda, the actress. But whether he will go ahead and succeed with his oft-expressed plan to buy the National Broadcasting Company from General Electric Company is uncertain at this writing.

Conrad Moffat Black. Black was born in Montreal in 1944 and earned his bachelor of arts degree at Carleton University in 1965, his law degree at Laval University in 1970 and a master's degree in history from McGill University. He could have pursued a career in either law or the teaching of history, but instead he developed a love for newspapers and in the next two decades he accumulated newspapers by the dozens. Between 1985 and 1990, he gained control of England's right-wing *Daily Telegraph*, the *Sunday Telegraph* and the *Spectator* weekly magazine. He also acquired a number of Canadian newspapers.

In the U.S., he collected more than a hundred dailies and weeklies in small cities and towns. But in 1994, he climaxed his American hunt by buying the *Chicago Sun-Times*, ending a century of ownership by the Marshall Field family. Operating from the Toronto headquarters of his Hollinger Inc., Black is often on the move keeping tabs on his properties everywhere.

"S.I." Newhouse, the legendary American newspaper acquirer, would probably more recognize and appreciate

Conrad Black than either Rupert Murdoch or Ted Turner because Black is almost exclusively a newspaper buyer.

The Entertainment-Plus Moguls: Redstone, Kerkorian, Kluge

Sumner Murray Redstone. No doubt much gratified that final week of August 1994 when Rand Araskog was preparing to hoist his ITT flag over Madison Square Garden, Redstone was a man on top of the world as the chairman of Viacom International. He had just sold Madison Square Garden which was owned by Paramount Communications, the entertainment-publishing empire he had recently acquired. And he was about to buy the Blockbuster Entertainment Corporation, the largest chain of video stores in the U.S. with no fewer than 3,755 of them in operation. To top it off, the sale of Madison Square Garden would help him pay for the Paramount acquisition.

It was all a heady time for a former lawyer, special assistant to the U.S. Attorney General, and law professor at Boston University. Redstone was born in 1923 in Boston and received his bachelor's and law degrees from Harvard. After some years of law practice, he became involved with National Amusements Inc., of Dedham, Massachusetts, was elected president and CEO in 1967 and chairman in 1986. He then became chairman of Viacom International, one of the biggest cable TV operators.

With his various acquisitions, Redstone emerged as one of the premier operators of media and entertainment systems in America, a rare example of a lawyer who can rise to a truly, lofty business position. Charitable and much involved in Jewish philanthropy, Redstone has plenty on his plate these days to occupy his fertile mind. Is he through with M&As for awhile, like Rand Araskog? Don't count on it. Wait for developments.

Kirk Kerkorian. This California takeover artist has a life story that could furnish the plot for several Hollywood movies, possibly for MGM which he acquired in the early 1970s. Kerkor Kerkorian was born in 1917, the grandson of Kasper Kerkorian who emigrated from Armenia to Detroit in 1890. With income earned on a farm, Kasper brought his son, Ahron, and Ahron's sweetheart, Lilly, to the U.S., where they had four children, including Kerkor, who later Americanized his name to Kirk. Ahron failed at one business after another. The family moved to Los Angeles in the vain hope that its fortunes would improve with the more provident weather.

In school, Kirk was rebellious, fighting, often truant. Expelled from one junior high school, he was transferred to another and then assigned to a high school which he left before graduating in order to help support the family. He worked at a variety of jobs and became an amateur boxer with a fine won-lost record. Taking a sample flying lesson, he decided it was just what he wanted and worked as a bouncer in a bar to earn money for flying lessons. He became a pilot on short-run, regional flights. During World War II, he was a captain in the British Royal Air Force Transport Command. After the war, Kerkorian opened a school for pilots in California and in the 1950s he started a business converting war-surplus military planes to commercial aircraft. He bought several DC-3's in Hawaii, flew them to California where they were overhauled and sold for six times what he paid for them. In 1960, he established Trans International Airlines from which he made a profit of $1.1 million in 1962. That year, he sold the airline to Studebaker Corporation and then after he expanded and improved the airline using Studebaker financial backing, he repurchased TIA. In 1969, he sold the airline to Transamerica Corporation, earning $104 million from the sale of his stock.

He was also investing in Las Vegas real-estate while gambling in its casinos. He loved the atmosphere and believed in Las Vegas' future. In 1968, he had bought the Flamingo Hotel for $12.5 million and then sold the land at a profit to a group that built Caesar's Palace on the site. In 1970, he bought Western Airlines. At the same time, he began accumulating the stock of Metro-Goldwyn-Mayer Corporation, and by 1974 owned 50.1 percent of the stock. He hired CBS's black sheep James T. Aubrey in 1969 to run MGM and fired him two years later for not making enough profitable films. Kerkorian named himself Aubrey's replacement. He built the 2,000-room MGM Grand Hotel in Las Vegas to be one of the city's showplaces.

But he ran into prolonged troubles at MGM, gave up the CEO's post to be executive committee chairman and tried to settle down. But it was not in his nature. He once told a reporter who asked why he kept buying, selling and building, "What do you want me to do? Sit on the veranda with a mint julep?"

Like Icahn, Boone Pickens and Ron Perelman, Kerkorian's name often crops up when merger rumors fly. I imagine that he likes that because the prospect tones him up professionally as physically he keeps trim playing tennis and lifting his bar-bells.

John Kluge. "Klug" in German means "clever" and it's quite apparent that that's what John Kluge was when in the 1950s he decided that television had a bright future even if one started small. In 1946, the German-born Kluge got his feet wet in the broadcasting business when he paid $15,000 for his first radio station, WGAY, in Silver Springs, Maryland. Then he became interested in and bought the Metropolitan Broadcasting Company, a tiny New York network with a handful of television stations. He renamed it Metromedia, took it public and expanded it into a major, independent complex of broadcasting, entertainment, advertising and sports. Eventually, it included television stations, radio stations, large, outdoor advertising companies, the Ice Capades and the Harlem Globetrotters, a motley mixture that made nothing but money.

Born in 1914 in Chemnitz, Germany, the son of an engineer, Kluge came to the United States at the age of 7 when his father died and his mother decided to leave Germany. They settled in Detroit where John worked for a while on an assembly line at the Ford Motor Company. After initial studies at Wayne State University in Detroit, he received a scholarship to attend Columbia University in New York. Upon graduation, he worked for Otten Brothers in Detroit as vice president and general manager. During World War II, he served in the U.S. Army as an intelligence captain. He used his Army discharge money to buy the radio station that launched him on his career.

Over time, Kluge made many acquisitions for Metromedia, often against the judgment of his financial advisors. But, though already inured to his willingness to take chances, many in the broadcasting industry were amazed when he borrowed

$1.2 billion in 1984 to buy all of Metromedia's stock in the largest leveraged buyout up till that point. He then sold almost all his properties to retire his debt but still amassed one of the nation's largest fortunes. "Taking a risk is where I get my kicks," he told an interviewer. "It's got my adrenaline going like crazy."

Reputedly worth between $6 billion and $8 billion, he was listed by Forbes as the wealthiest American in 1989, 1990 and 1991. But he remembered his alma mater and his humble beginnings by donating $25 million to Columbia to aid minority youth.

In more recent years, instead of retiring, Kluge has been building a new empire, mostly through acquisitions. It consists of restaurant chains (Ponderosa, Bennington's, Bonanza and Steak & Ale); LDDS Metromedia Communications, a long-distance telephone carrier; Stanodyne Automotive, an auto products manufacturer; lodging businesses; Orion Pictures and technological businesses.

Is that it from Kluge? At 80 years old it could be. But for a player who gets his kicks from taking risks—is there a more successful one?—age is no real factor. Like the advertising theme of a famous brand of alkaline battery, he will probably keep going and going.

The Acquisition Moguls: Araskog, Pickens, Icahn, and Perelman

Rand V. Araskog. Cool, disciplined but determined, the chairman and chief executive officer of ITT Corporation inherited the mantle and seat of the fabled Harold Geneen, the once-upon-a-time king of mergers who built ITT into the "operator of 250 companies." But Araskog, a West Point graduate and medium big wheel of the Defense Department in the 1950s, promptly began dismantling ITT as if he were king of divestiture. Finally, by the end of the 1980s, he had whittled the company down to just a handful of principal units, Sheraton Hotels, Harford Fire insurance, financial services and manufactured products. Although the company in 1993 bought the Desert Inn Hotel and Casino in Las Vegas from Kirk Kerkorian, it had not been a big merger player in recent years. So were Araskog and ITT largely opting out of the merger game, secure in its $23 billion sales?

That idea, if it was ever valid, was dashed late in August 1994 when ITT and Cablevision Systems, which operates cable TV networks in 19 states, combined to buy Madison Square Garden in New York and its assorted assets including the New York Knicks professional basketball and New York Rangers hockey teams. Why the entry into the sports business? Araskog was petulant at the question asked at a press conference. "Four years ago, I said that entertainment and leisure times was one area we could get going in," he replied. "We feel this fits with our Sheraton operations and gives us a new approach with a strong partner. To suggest that this is capricious is an insult." He almost had to act indignant. ITT was paying $600 million of its $700-$800 million cash kitty as its share of the $1.07 billion purchase price, much more than Cablevision's contribution.

Araskog was born in Fergus Falls, Minnesota in 1931, graduated from West Point in 1953 and took postgraduate work at Harvard in 1958 and 1959. He was with the Defense Department from 1954 until 1959, rising to special assistant to the director in the last two years. Marketing director for Honeywell Corporation's aerospace division from 1960 to 1970, he jointed ITT as a vice president in 1971. Eighteen years later, he became its president and chief executive officer as Geneen's heir apparent and in 1990 he also became its chairman. He may have been Geneen's antithesis in divesting ITT of hundreds of companies. But in terms of mergers, he showed that he learned at the hands of the master.

Not long after the Madison Square Garden deal, in December 1994, ITT announced its purchase of Caesars World, one of the premiere casinos in Las Vegas, for $1.7 billion. The move gave ITT an opportunity not merely to underscore its major role in the gaming industry with two major casinos but ultimately to add gaming to its Sheraton Hotels wherever it could around the world.

Thomas Boone Pickens. A wildcatter who became a greenmail expert and corporate raider, "Boone" Pickens was born in 1928 in Holdenville, Oklahoma and earned a bachelor's degree in geology at Oklahoma State University in 1951. That year he joined Phillips Petroleum in Bartlesville, Oklahoma, as a geologist. But he soon began to look at the big oil companies as enemies. They were selfish, greedy and morally unworthy of their high position, he told friends and anyone who would listen. This attitude launched him on an unusual career as a business populist who nonetheless could make many millions for himself and his associates by the simple tactic of compelling big oil companies to pay him back for the stock that he accumulated to threaten them.

After he left Phillips, he wildcatted on his own and found several oil gushers which provided the stake to start his own Mesa Petroleum Company in Amarillo, Texas, in 1964. He quickly ran up its sales to $400 million. More important, Mesa became his invasion base. As a target, he zeroed in on oil company reserves as more valuable than generally supposed and urged that the big refiners sell them and distribute the proceeds to their shareholders. This hardly endeared him to Big Oil but suddenly he was a stockholder's advocate, too.

In 1976, he launched his first takeover move. He made a $22-a-share offer for Aztec Oil and Gas Company but naively failed to buy any of its shares in advance. When another company got Aztec, Pickens had no stock in it to bargain with or profit from. It was a lesson he never forgot. His next offensive against Cities Service Company was more productive. Even though he was outbid by Gulf Oil Corporation. Pickens netted $40 million for Mesa by selling Cities the stock he had squirreled away.

Next came General American Oil Company, a well-established, independent oil and gas concern. Pickens bought a sizeable block of stock and notified the company of his plan to make a bid for all of it. But General American's investment bankers convinced Phillips Petroleum, Pickens' old employer, to come in as a white knight with a higher bid. Pickens dropped out again, this time earning another profit of $45 million for Mesa. By that time, though excited by his greenmail earnings, he decided that he loved the push-and-shove game of mergers even more. This time, he happily went after Phillips

Petroleum and once more intensified the merger fever that gripped the oil industry, largely because of his unflagging zeal. He didn't get Phillips. But he did get $89 million in greenmail while his faceoff with Phillips boosted the stock for its shareholders.

There is something pixyish-evangelical in Pickens' blue eyes, sandy hair and wiry, relaxed form. He never minded bragging about his greenmailing skills but it was very obvious that he enjoyed the game of attack, conquer or withdraw with rich booty. I met him once in New York and was impressed by the clear but piercing gaze that he directed at the world. Of average stature and build, he emits a quiet confidence which makes one wonder what he's really after. Judging by his feats, I think he get tremendous joy from making money by outwitting the big guys in oil while irritating them in the bargain with his calls for corporate democracy. He's one of those few people who have those two normally opposing strains—wealth and idealism. In 1984, according to Forbes Magazine, he was the highest-paid U.S. executive, earning $20 million that year.

He may be of an older generation of big merger players but his name still crops up as a potential hostile-or-greenmail player.

Carl Icahn. Like Boone Pickens, this adept greenmailer and corporate invader has a deceptive exterior. When I first met him during one of his many quixotic tilts with the establishment, it was on Madison Avenue in Manhattan. One of his lieutenants who knew me stood on a corner with Icahn, called me over and introduced me. I didn't quite know how to take Icahn. He had the misty, soulful face of a mystic and the stooped, gangling posture of someone not quite sure of himself. But that initial appraisal could not have been more wrong. He was a tough, practical visionary, educated in philosophy but honed on Wall Street. As he became more successful, his stoop disappeared.

He was born in Queens, New York City, in 1936. His father was a lawyer and sometime cantor in the local synagogue. Carl earned a bachelor's degree in philosophy at Princeton, started his career on Wall Street in the 1960s and opened his own stock brokerage in 1968, making money for friends and clients.

A decade later, he gave up simple investing for corporate takeovers. In 1979, he gained control of Baird & Water, a Chicago real-estate investment trust, which became Bayswater Realty and Investment Trust in honor of his Queens neighborhood. Soon after, he learned the joys of greenmailing as had Boone Pickens. His record in the next few years in greenmailing made him and his partners wealthy: Tappan Company, $2.7 million; Hammermill Paper, $9 million; Marshall Field & Company, $30 million; Phillips Petroleum, $50 million.

Icahn's greatest triumph was his 1985 hostile bid for TWA, the once powerful but then troubled airline. He succeeded in taking it over but it turned into a protracted and massive headache. At heart, he remained a risk-taker and happy greenmailer. Besides studying philosophy, he became an adept chess-player and this "allows me to think rationally," he said once. So while grappling with TWA's problems as its CEO, he apparently felt it rational for him to make a sidewise stab at Viacom International. He walked away with a $40 million profit.

Ronald Owen Perelman. As an MBA, combining an indomitable belief in himself and a zest for surprises, Perelman won the Revlon Group, the big cosmetics company, in a hostile takeover in 1985 and became its chairman and CEO. After growing up in Greensboro, North Carolina, he received his education at the University of Pennsylvania with a bachelor's degree in 1964 and an MBA at the university's Wharton School in 1966. After a start in another firm, he became chairman and CEO of MacAndrews & Forbes Holdings, Wilmington, Delaware, an investment company which became the base from which he went after such companies as Salomon Brothers, Pantry Pride supermarkets and Revlon.

In his forays at those three companies, he lost out at Salomon because Warren Buffett, the much respected investor, took a stake in that investment banking house that precluded an outside takeover. But Perelman snapped up Pantry Pride in Philadelphia. However, when he came at Revlon as the not-very-credible CEO of a supermarket chain, many on Wall Street laughed at the prospect. But Perelman won Revlon after a tough fight, using a mass of junk bonds which encouraged other takeover artists to do likewise.

Perelman, like Rupert Murdoch, is often viewed as the bogeyman who just might jump into any situation where a company is in "play." He's a fearless competitor, able to plunge through to victory even as everyone predicts that he doesn't have the money or the crust to do so. He has proven that he's got both.

The LBO Moguls: Kravis and Forstmann

Henry R. Kravis. One of the foremost venture financiers of his time, Kravis as the senior partner of Kohlberg, Kravis & Roberts is America's best-known practitioner of the leveraged buyout. His greatest claim to fame is his 1986 LBO of RJR Nabisco, a $30 billion transaction which, as mentioned earlier, was a disappointment in return on investment, eventual stock price and lack of synergy. His effort to recoup from this major setback was generally viewed as the reason why in 1994 he made a bold and successful move to acquire control of the Borden Company, a formerly powerful food products maker then wallowing in inertia and uncertain leadership. Using the common stock of RJR Holdings, Kravis parlayed a pile of low-value stock into a takeover of Borden.

An unusual mixture of an outgoing personality and an occasional disdain for other financial players, Kravis was born in Tulsa, Oklahoma, in 1944, went to private schools in Massachusetts and Connecticut and took a job briefly in the mail room of Sunray DX Oil Company in Tulsa. He made his mark early. At the Loomis School in Connecticut, he was captain of the wrestling team and vice president of the student council. But then and later, he always seemed to be thrusting his way up against the bigger students and athletes. It's likely that his role model was his father, Raymond, the son of an English tailor who had emigrated to Atlantic City, New Jersey. A very successful investor, Raymond lost it all in the Crash of 1929 and then made a second fortune as a petroleum engineer.

While Henry was an economics undergraduate at Claremont College in California, his father got him a job summers at Goldman Sachs in New York. There he learned some of the ways of Wall Street but he left after graduation for the Madison Fund where he helped to locate hot stocks for the respected money management firm. Madison, which owned Katy Industries, a regional railroad, was impressed enough with the young Kravis to assign him to diversify Katy's operations. He did so and did it well but a few years later the company was sold.

With the help of George Roberts, his cousin, Kravis got a job at Bear Stearns, working for Jerome Kohlberg, head of corporate finance. These, as it turned out, were Henry's potential partners. In 1965, Kohlberg was already an expert in LBOs, and Kravis learned at his shoulder as Kohlberg engineered one deal after another to help aging entrepreneurs. Using borrowed money, these men could still hang on to their companies as minor investors while squirreling away the proceeds from the sales of their businesses. Kohlberg also snapped up the cast-off divisions of the troubled, weary conglomerates. All this Henry Kravis absorbed through his pores. Soon, he was trying to out-think and outperform his boss Kohlberg.

Kohlberg decided to leave Bear Stearns when it refused to start a separate LBO division and he was joined in the new firm by both Kravis and Roberts. It was 1977 and not the best of times for a new venture capital company because of an uncertain market and travail at some of the big investment houses. Things were lean for the first few years but broke open in 1981, with six completed transactions. Still, Kohlberg Kravis & Roberts was a puny contender in a market dominated by the likes of Merrill Lynch, Goldman Sachs, Drexel Burnham and Salomon Brothers. But each deal they made was larger than the previous one. The partners, all very dedicated to their own convictions, fought bitterly with one another. But there was no gainsaying their greatest triumphs, such as acquiring Safeway Stores, one of the nation's largest food chains, not to mention the dramatic, if badly conceived, RJR Nabisco deal. The partnership broke up when Jerry Kohlberg resigned after his two partners insisted that he was no longer pulling his weight and was no longer entitled to his equal share of the business.

It was a bitter end to a productive relationship in which Kohlberg had taught the two younger men much and helped them become rich. Kravis meanwhile had come to love the happy life of jet set society and had married Carolyne Roehm, the attractive, fashion designer. He was on top of the world when he made his successful stab at RJR Nabisco but ran afoul of Ted Forstmann, who also wanted RJR. It proved to be the fight of his life but Kravis came out on top.

Theodore J. Forstmann. Founder and top man of his own LBO firm, Forstmann Little & Company, Ted Forstmann was a proud, intense venture capitalist whose company already owned businesses with sales amounting to more than $9 billion. He disliked Henry Kravis because he considered him a man playing with "funny money," i.e., the junk bonds fostered by Michael Milken. Forstmann despised junk bonds. Some Wall Streeters thought that Forstmann was just jealous of Kravis. But Ted insisted that Kravis had fostered the junk bond trend that had so hurt the financial community. In other words, Kravis' technique of composing takeover bids consisted of a minimum of cash and a maximum of very risky, high-interest junk bonds. That, Ted insisted, was no way to buy a company. And the more companies that Kravis bought that way, the angrier Forstmann got.

He was born in 1941 to a famous textile family whose company, Forstmann Woolens, had made its members wealthy and its name respected in the U.S. and abroad. Ted grew up in Greenwich, Connecticut, played tennis on the mansion's courts and by the time he was 16 was ranked as a top amateur player. When his father died, Ted tried to fulfill his parent's wish that he go to law school and enrolled at Columbia Law School. But the Forstmann Woolens business had entered a period of stagnation, almost failed and then was sold. Ted helped pay for his Columbia tuition by exercising his skill at cards, often winning at bridge from wealthy men who didn't mind losing several hundred dollars a night at a game they loved.

He worked briefly after graduation for a New York law firm, hated the menial research assignments he was given and finally left for Wall Street. Henry Kravis was one of Ted's co-workers at a firm on Wall Street in the 1970s. But Ted wandered away from the firm in search of a job that would not be confining or compel him to take orders. His first break came when he convinced the president of a company to allow him to sell it. He did sell it and earned $300,000 in fees from it. Attracting attention this way, he found several investors willing to back him in his own company. He would do LBOs but without junk bonds, he told them, relying instead on more traditional and tried financing. He and Brian Little, an investment banker, started the firm in 1978. Like Kohlberg Kravis & Roberts, Forstmann Little convinced pension funds to invest in deals which gave the LBO firm an immense pool of funds to draw from.

Pushing hard, travelling the country to shake hands and spread the word, Ted helped his firm not only buy and sell businesses for others but also for his company. In 1983, it outbid others to acquire the Dr Pepper soft-drink business. But Forstmann Little a few years later found itself unable to compete when the great tide of LBOs pushed bid prices higher and higher and out of its reach. Still, there were lulls even in the LBO market and in one of them the firm acquired another solid company, the Lear Siegler Company, a respected defense contractor. But Kohlberg Kravis & Roberts always seemed a step ahead of him. And so, with KKR jumping in and out of deals like a jack-rabbit, Ted Forstmann sometimes wondered if he weren't asleep at the switch but his overall record was a good one.

Kravis' offensive at RJR Nabisco presented an intriguing opportunity for Forstmann to show up the flashy Kravis and gain plaudits as "an honest financier." Only KKR once again outflanked him and outbid him and all he could do after the RJR incident was fume some more and stick verbal pins into his enemy.

Those are my dozen big players. Is there something to be said about any common denominators that make them tick?

I've already described them as "tough." But they are also resilient, big in approach, courageous, indomitable, innovative, hyperenergetic. And also difficult, extremely demanding, not particularly sensitive to other people's needs, impatient and often impossible. The fact is that it's hard to like them as a group but also hard to dislike them. They have to be watched, though, because they might just buy your business, your house, and maybe your car out from under you.

Are they—the *Big* question—America's new entrepreneurs?

They are, or people just like them.

chapter 11

The Little Players

He was a victim of a basic American dilemma. "You start a business, work very hard at it for a long time, build it up and then what? Endless, grinding hours, no family succession, a bleak future?" The owner of the security company located in southeastern Pennsylvania was very candid.

"You see, it's this way. My wife and I are breaking our backs working 80 hours a week," he told Jim Throne, a local business broker. "I built this business up to $1 million in volume but we've got a central facility that can handle up to $5 million in sales. On one hand, we're ready to take off. On the other hand, we want to sell our company. I think we can get $5 million. A venture capital company wants to invest $1.5 million with us for a 25 percent interest. Our private investors might be induced to cough up some money if I ask them. But I really want to do something else."

Throne, a former businessman himself, understood the man's dilemma. He, too, had been working with his wife in his own business in Stewartstown, Pennsylvania, for the last 14 years. "I told the security man that I would try to come up with two proposals," he related. "I would recommend one but not the other. But he could decide which appealed to him more."

The Business of Brokering

In hamlets, towns, small and big cities across America, the business brokers are on the move. Whether they are in their offices hovering over a computer, hurrying to appointments around town or barrelling down the highways to other cities, thousands of business brokers around the country are busily putting sellers and buyers together. And they are busy. More than 250,000 small- or medium-sized American businesses change hands every year. But unlike the bigger company deals, they draw little publicity and attention even though in the small cities and towns collectively they may have a greater impact than the movements of larger companies.

Starting in 1993, the turnover tempo among small companies intensified as a result of an improved economy and a more optimistic outlook among businessmen. Manufacturing companies predominate in these turnovers but as the United States reacts to significant demographic and economic shifts in urban, suburban and rural areas, there is scarcely a single type of business that isn't being bought or sold.

The dimensions of the small merger-and-acquisition process obviously are much more modest than those of the big deals. Prices are much lower, rarely topping $15 million, and the terms are simpler reflecting the smaller price tag. In the larger transactions, strategic motivation is an important factor; in the modest transactions personal reasons assume a greater role, as in the case of the Pennsylvania security company. Those reasons, not necessarily in order of importance, are personal boredom, declining health, the reluctance of the second generation to continue the business, and desperation caused by poor business or an unfavorable economy.

Since most small businesses represent an individual entrepreneur, terms of the deal—the type of non-cash to be included and the length of the payout—are much more important than in the case of the corporate seller. Many pending small deals languish over terms because the founder wants out as quickly as possible, thinks himself very mortal or is just impatient. That's why, contrary to popular thought, the selling price is much less important in small company sales than the matter of terms.

What is a "small business" and what selling price can it command? "Ninety-five percent of small businesses gross under $500,000 in annual sales," says Tom West, president of the International Business Brokers Association, a trade group based in Concord, Massachusetts. "The average price they draw is about $150,000."

While the average broker operates on a small scale, often as a one-man business, a number around the country have large staffs, franchise their operations or set up partnerships. Since it is an entrepreneurial activity requiring a knowledge of business operations, marketing and finance, the vast majority of business brokers come from other fields where they have acquired experience. For many it is a second, even a third career. But to give it legitimacy, the IBBA will approve an individual as a "certified business intermediary" after he or she completes a number of required courses.

No doubt as a sign of the times, a growing number of retired senior citizens are returning to work as business brokers, putting their lengthy experience to good use and no longer sitting it out.

The following interviews present a flavor of brokering in various regions of the U.S.

Geneva Companies: The Biggest of the Little

In the Geneva Companies headquarters in Irvine, California, and in branch offices in New York, Chicago and Clearwater, Florida, brokers, associates, statisticians and clericals pummel a list of 15,000 confirmed buyers, 400 on-line databases and the research efforts of a 15-person information group into a drive to line up sellers with buyers and arrange successful transactions. Almost all of their work is on behalf of a selling company and the quest for a buyer is pressed with a full marketing campaign as if it were a product launch.

"We're the largest merger-and-acquisition company serving mid-market clients, or those with a market value of from $1 million to $100 million," says Stephen Chrisham, executive vice president of Geneva Business Services, one of the Geneva companies. "We have 350 managing directors and deal-makers and we operate all four of our offices. We do not franchise."

After the recession in 1990 and 1991, there's been an uptrend in middle-market mergers and acquisitions, reflecting an improved, national economy and a more optimistic view of the future by most businessmen, Chrisham says. "We find that the environment has brightened for industry in general," he adds. "The fear of an economic downturn has faded."

Is there a formula that sets the price of a sale? "There isn't any," he replies. "That's why we market all transactions without a price. We do this in order to place the acquirer in a competitive, bidding situation to get the best price for our client. We tell the potential buyer, 'We'll give you the information on the company. You visit with them and if you like it, tell us what you think it is worth. Tell us the price and the structure or terms. We will have others, too. But we won't beat you over the head.'"

Geneva Companies, founded in 1977, holds occasional seminars to build its client list, which mostly includes selling companies in manufacturing, wholesaling, and retailing. But the primary ones are manufacturers with a proprietary product in such industries as food, consumer packaged items, health-care and medicine."Naturally, the most desirable companies sell the quickest," Chrisham says. "But basically, everything is selling with varying degrees of swiftness." Unlike other but smaller brokers, he was unwilling to indicate how many deals Geneva concludes a year because he considers the information competitive.

Locating a buyer entails a "broad, marketing effort. We take the company that will be sold and put together a marketing plan by describing the client fully," Chrisham says. "We distribute it through all our offices because buyers can be located anywhere. We identify potential buyers but that certainly isn't restrictive. We use every database that we can. We find that our buyer list has grown constantly over the years."

"The main motivation for selling a business nowadays is boredom," he says. "It's by far the overriding factor followed by health problems."

On a personal basis, as with most other business brokers interviewed, Chrisham had a prior business career. Before joining Geneva in 1984, he worked for several firms as head of product marketing and was a strategic marketing consultant.

Jim Throne of Pennsylvania

"I told the man with the security company he wanted to sell that he could consider two proposals," Jim Throne said. "One would be a strategic partner, say, a larger company in an allied business which can see a growth potential in combining its company with his. That company would have the ability to pay the seller on an earn-out basis while he continues to work there for a few more years. But it would have to be a pretty good deal for the seller. He says that his company is doing very well and can earn $2 million over two years."

The second proposal he gave the client was that they could find a company to buy his outright, "pay what it thinks it is worth and just take it over. It would not be a partner as the other would be. The client could take his money and run. But I told him that this is a lesser possibility for him."

In Stewartstown, a suburb of York, Pennsylvania, the economy has picked up and Jim Throne and his wife, who works closely with him, have enjoyed two good years. "We consider ourselves an investment banking firm but you can call us what you like. We handle mid-sized companies, the selling prices of which go from $1 million to as much as $75 million but the majority wind up at about the $1 million level."

Most of Throne's clients are sellers who are generally in manufacturing as well as in distributing and the service business. One pervading reason makes many of them want to sell their businesses. "It's the fact that the owner or major stockholder feels he has reached the peak that he can handle and that it is getting beyond him," Throne said. "He can't handle a major business. He's losing control. In many cases, he's also failed to install a second tier of management, because he has to control everything but it's gone beyond him and it's too late."

Another reason is that the company needs financing in order to grow but the owner has problems arranging for it. "Even if a company is uniquely positioned and can grow, the owner has to demonstrate that the growth can be handled in order to get the financing and in a good many cases that is impossible," Throne said.

He and his wife each complete three transactions a year, working on a retainer, out-of-pocket expenses and a fee based on a percentage of the sale price. "The broker business looks easier from the outside than it is," he says. "A lot of people want to get into it but the sales cycle takes a long time. The bigger-brokered deals turn faster."

A descendant of a German family that emigrated to the United States in 1732, Throne was president of his family's building materials company until it was sold in 1979. A year later, he became a broker with another man as partner. They had offices both in York and in Towson, Maryland, but the partnership lasted only one year. "After commuting back and forth between York and Towson for a dozen years," he said, "I moved my business into a single office on Main Street in Stewartstown. I'm happy here. It's my hometown. I know everyone."

Herb Cohen of New York

Now 60 years old, Herb Cohen has been a business broker, or in "fancier language, an intermediary," for the last decade in upstate New York. Before that, he was a commercial real-estate broker. "Most of us in the business broker field were something else first," he said. "It's a relatively new business, formally, that is. If you're over 40, you predate the brokerage business as it is today."

The big change in his professional life came in 1986 when new Federal tax legislation changed the rule that a passive investor could take a loss on his investment, as in tax shelters.

In one big step, it removed the advantage he, his associates and their investors had for remaining in real-estate investments. He was effectively out of business and started looking for a new one.

"At about the same time," he relates, "a friend of mine wanted to sell his business and invited some professionals in who came over with a tape measure and proceeded to make some superficial estimates of his assets. He thought it would take more than that. I did, too. I told him to give me his last few years' tax returns and operating statements. I went to work on them and on finding a buyer. I finally came up with a live one and a price that was higher than he had imagined. He became a real fan. He told me, 'There must be a lot more people like me who want to sell. Why don't you go after them?'"

In 1986, he joined the firm of Robert A. Mead, Inc., a diversified brokerage in Vestal, New York, near Binghamton. He also earned the "C.B.I." designation for "certified business intermediary" by completing courses offered by the International Business Brokers Association. Over the next few years, he sold many businesses, including machine shops, restaurants, dental practices, and funeral homes. "My last closing was an electroplating plant," he said. "You can see why I don't get bored. The diversity of assignments keeps me interested."

Observant, articulate, and analytical, Cohen has enjoyed, not to mention profited by some interesting experiences. He's enough of a spectator to sit back at times, too, and wonder what makes people, small businessmen, in particular, tick. He relates a recent experience along those lines.

"Usually, a small entrepreneur isn't very meticulous or accurate about the books he keeps. But I had one fellow come in with the most beautiful sets of books I've ever seen," Cohen said. "It was obvious that he wanted to sell his business from strength. I was impressed. Now I think one of the reasons small businessmen aren't great on keeping their books is that they tend to skim off the business and I accept that as a given. But I tell such people that skimming is like eating a piece of cake. When you eat it, it ain't no more. You can't sell what isn't there anymore. So don't expect that a careless book, with holes in it, will help you sell your business. And that's why I was so taken with this guy who was willing to show such clean, neat books to a complete stranger. It was all there documented with no loopholes."

Cohen also has been working with a number of out-placement firms which are trying to assist displaced executives from some of the country's biggest corporations. Several of the out-placement clients have asked Cohen to help them buy a small business but they have only the most meager knowledge of what their investment will be able to produce. "I've found some of these executives looking to be entrepreneurs tell me they're willing to invest from $25,000 to $50,000 in a tiny business," said Cohen, "but they want at least that much back in profits at the end of a year or two."

"Well, what would you tell them?" Cohen was asked. "I don't know what you would say but I told him, 'Listen, if I find a business like that for you, I won't sell it. I'll buy it myself.'"

Not many executives who walk away from big companies with the classical "golden parachute" possess entrepreneurial talent or spirit, says Herb Cohen. As a case in point, he cites a former machine-shop director for one of America's largest corporations, who, after being let go, wanted to buy a machine shop of his own. "Now it happened that I had just that kind of business on tap," he said, "and the client said he was very interested. I put the two of them together and it looked good. They spent some time talking together and the machine-shop owner gave the executive a tour and a rundown on the whole facility, its equipment and its operation. After the tour, we went into the owner's office and sat for a while. Suddenly, the potential buyer said, 'Herb, let's go.'

"I was very puzzled because it had looked so good. But as we stood outside, the executive said, 'Who does the buying, the selling, the office work and everything else?' Naturally, I told him, 'The owner, of course. He keeps busy all the time because he has a very small staff.' Well, my client's face fell. It was clear what was troubling him. Working as an executive in a very large corporation, he had lots of other people doing all those things. He never had to worry about them until he was confronted by them. There was only one bit of advice that I could give him. 'Maybe you ought to get a partner.' I said."

A graduate of Cornell University with a bachelor's degree in economics, Cohen earned an advanced degree in 1959 at Syracuse University. In 1993 when a group of individuals formed the New York State Association of Business Brokers, he became its president.

"I like to do a deal a month," he said. "My present listing goes from an asking price of $100,000 to under $5 million. I basically represent the sellers but I do searches for buyers and I also do business evaluations for clients who want them. I always maintain a file of motivated buyers, who have been qualified. If a business would be better served through cooperation with other sources, I participate in an active network of business brokers within New York State, nationwide and even worldwide."

John Keate of Ohio

Prototypically American, a hard-working, midwest mechanic started a truck parts manufacturing business a quarter-century ago and enjoyed watching it grow into a multi-million dollar business with 80 employees. But when it expanded to 250 employees and $25 million in sales, he decided that the fun had gone out of it. He felt he was still a mechanic and thrived most in a start-up situation. "I never had any management training," he admitted, "and I don't think I've got any talent for it."

He asked J. S. Keate & Company in Cincinnati, Ohio, to handle the sale of his company. "We have just started the selling process," said John Keate, head of the brokerage, "but we've already gotten quite a bit of interest in it from larger companies. Unlike some other brokers, we went to market with the price up front. We expect to get $5 million. At that level, we give the price up front to winnow out those that can't handle it. On expected sales of $1 million, we go to market without price. We just might get a better offer that way."

With eight on his staff, four partners and four associates—"like a law firm"—the company does 30 to 50 deals a year. "We get a retainer but no expenses and an accomplishment fee of from 2 percent to 12 percent of the purchase price," Keate says. "The highest percentage is on the smaller deals and it goes down as the deal price goes up. The retainer, of course, comes out of it."

The Keate brokers sell businesses for prices up to $10 million. Clients range widely from a Main Street dry-cleaner to a manufacturing firm. "Business in 1994 has been up. In fact, the market is very good," says Keate. "The economy is very good in the Midwest. Banks are more cooperative. And I think there is some pent-up demand to sell in a better economy and get a better price. We are getting better prices now, although it's a little tougher to close a deal because of the Federal regulations on business, like the rules from the Environmental Protection Agency.

"But, in general, things are picking up in our business after a slow 1991 through 1993," Keate says. "1990 was our peak year."

Burnout and boredom are the main reasons why small businessmen decide to sell, he says. "There's also retirement and health problems and, I think, less of a desire on the part of the owner to turn the business over to the second generation. The net worth of the owner is tied up in the business and he doesn't want to lose it."

Keate adds that he receives referrals from accountants, attorneys and businessmen and also works with other brokers on certain deals. The "multiple listing" can bring in a bonanza, he says, in combination with a thorough marketing procedure.

He tells the story of a computer reseller company which Keate represented with the assistance of other brokers outside the Cincinnati area.

"We ultimately received offers ranging from $500,000 to $1 million. But if the seller had only worked with one bidder, he would have left a lot of money on the table," Keate said. "So using the other brokers along with our marketing plan helped him. We used a confidential, controlled campaign to get broad exposure. We sent 350 letters to prospective buyers, giving details on the company but without naming it. Then we checked on the buyers who responded to see if they had the financial capability to handle the deal. Then we gave them a memo, finally identifying the company and asked them to sign a confidentiality agreement. We find that the competitive aspect of this process drives up the value of the property."

After graduating from the Cornell University School of Hotel Management, Keate bought a chain of discotheques, sold it in 1981 and then bought a broker franchise. He gave that up three years later to open his own broker's business.

Dick Read of Florida

In Orlando, Florida, the land of sun, Disneyworld and tanned retirees, Dick Read has built a brokerage of 11 agents who do 30 transactions in an average year and as many as 50 in a strong one. Read, a former general manager for various manufacturing firms, started in the business brokerage field eight-and-a-half years ago. "I worked for companies making such things as decorative aluminum parts or portable toilets for boats, trailers or recreational vehicles," he said. "But I got tired of working for a boss and I bought a franchise in a brokerage network."

His immediate employment at the time was in Michigan and he preferred to have his franchise there. But the franchisor told him that the territory was already covered. Instead, he could have Orlando if he wished. So Read sold his house, moved to the Orlando area and settled in a suburb called Altamonte Springs. He soon found that his background as a moving force in the companies he had worked for came into good use in his own business.

"I've got 11 agents now. I know there is a trend in our business for smaller offices," says Read, "but I wanted a bigger scale operation. We've been busy. The trend is up around here. Orlando has been a good market with a sound economy. A lot of people who come down here want to buy a business. That includes company executives who were transferred to the Orlando area and were supposed to be transferred again but decided that they wanted to stay here."

He added, "We deal in businesses that don't need much expertise, like gas stations with convenience stores and dry-cleaners. We sold many video stores but now the big boys have them and they're not much of a market for us."

In addition to normal brokerage assignments, Read and his staff are getting an increasing number of fee-based work assignments such as preparing a portfolio "packaging" a business. Some of these lead to selling assignments. Consulting assignments, too, are growing, Read says. "Sometimes a buyer will come to us to finalize a deal that he has started and we will help him out," he says. "But those are strictly consulting jobs on an hourly basis in contrast to a full transaction."

Some of Read's staff of brokers are retirees who are now involved in their second or third careers. "They got tired of being retired," Read says. "They want to do something else with their lives. I'm glad to have them."

Read said, "Our outlook is good. The brokering business is maturing. It's becoming more professional and formalized. I like that."

Duncan Haile of Connecticut

In his neck of the Connecticut and the nearby New England market, Duncan Haile sees a constantly increasing number of new clients but many are potential buyers rather than sellers. "How secure is any job these days?" asks Haile, who operates C.D. Peterson Associates, a brokerage in Danbury, Connecticut. "That's why franchising, with all its problems, continues to attract people and why we find so many more people are looking for businesses."

In contrast to many brokers who favor representing only sellers, Read focuses exclusively on buyers. He finds it questionable from a moral standpoint to represent both. "It's difficult to work both sides of the fence. Besides, I think it's a conflict of interest," he asserts. "I find it more gratifying to work with buyers. If I work for a seller, each one will be drastically different. That would mean that I would have to constantly revisit the universe of buyers. But if I work for a buyer, I think I can focus better on potential sellers."

Everything is for sale for "the right price and the right payout structure," Haile says.

"But there is no such thing as an easy deal," he says. "I used to have a larger operation but it became a complex business. I decided to 'skinny down' and be an individual entrepreneur. It's more cost effective," he says. "It's also very difficult to teach someone else the business. Being an intermediary or broker, if you prefer, doesn't follow a pattern because there are so many companies on the buying side."

He works with a gamut of businesses from "Mom 'n Pop" (or call them "street") businesses up to manufacturers. Haile completes fewer than a half-dozen deals a year, but "they can cover a range including medical services or product suppliers, a distributorship, a retailer or an advertising business." To understand the nuances of each takes some solid effort, Haile says, but it's vital because it's the prerequisite to an "elaborate" process of exchanging information and consultation, not the least of which is acting as the client's advisor.

As brokering has evolved and grown, the number of more formalized buying groups has grown, too, he says. But their rise and competitive activity have compelled them to lower their sights somewhat, moving down from more lucrative deals to more average ones. "It's a matter of supply and demand," Haile says. "Everyone's more interested in the bigger, more profitable transactions but there are so many more smaller businesses than big ones."

Haile came to brokering more prepared than many others. Now 51 years old and a broker for the last 10 years, he is a former director of business development for the Timex Corporation, the world's largest watch producer. After 10 years with Timex, Haile worked as a corporate turnaround consultant. He started brokering in 1984 with Peter Peterson, who had been in the business for some time and they worked together as partners until Peterson's retirement.

A Californian who lived in New York before the Danbury venture, Haile, like Herb Cohen, points out that outplaced corporate executives in the New England area are eager to buy small businesses. But many are running into caution on the part of banks. "Banks want as much owner financing put into a deal as they can get," Haile says. "That's playing a big part in these smaller deals. If anything, banks are more cautious so that it's critical that buyers put their own money into deals, the more the better. Moreover, the banks like the bigger transactions. It's more interesting to them and the return is bigger."

Brian Knight of Vermont

With 10 offices in New England and on Canada's Atlantic Ocean coastline, "Country Businesses, Inc.," of Manchester, Vermont, is a broker powerhouse. It completes about 35 transactions a year, 20 percent of them in the hospitality field. The range of deals is broad.

"We completed a $15 million purchase of a wholesale auto parts distributor with some stores," says Brian Knight, president of Country Businesses. "It was one of our biggest transactions since we did a $30 million sale for a manufacturer of turbine engines. Then we also did a $150,000 deal of a deli. Nearly all of these deals are referred to us by accountants and lawyers. We almost always work only with sellers."

Country Businesses has a far higher success rate than other brokerages because it will estimate the price of a property, go to market with it and short-cut the sales process, Knight says. "We evaluate a business before we accept an assignment, to be fair to both the buyer and seller," he says. "By doing that, of course, we have to run down some seller-clients because the owners want more money than we think they can get. But we have a 75 percent success rate, because we cut out the potentially unproductive bidders by setting a market price in advance and we are more restrictive in choice."

Sellers usually want cash for their companies, Knight says, but are often compelled to accept a "structured" deal which means terms. And "it's the structure, not the price, that makes or breaks the deal," he says. He gave the following scenario of a transaction with structural "iffiness."

A buyer will make a down payment on the business he likes, amounting to between one-and-a-half to two-and-a-half times the company's historical cash flow.

The bank involved extends a loan of 60 percent to 75 percent of the appraised value of the "hard" assets of the business, not of its earnings.

The seller now has to "take back" a note for the portion of the selling price remaining from the combination of the bank loan and the buyer's deposit.

But the seller may not want to do that. If he or she hopes to get $1 million for the business and the assets are worth $400,000, the bank will extend $300,000. The cash flow was $100,000 in the prior year so the buyer must pay $200,000 up front. Together, that's only half the price the seller wants. Does the seller want to "structure" half of the deal? Will the bank go further? Is the buyer willing to extend more? These are the difficult questions that make a deal's "structure" the big hurdle, Knight says.

A New England affiliate of the Geneva Companies, Country Businesses is enjoying a business boom as the New England economy undergoes a revitalization, says Knight, who was also the 1994 president of the International Business Brokers Association. "There was a great deal of negative publicity about New England," he adds, "so the buyers disappeared and most businesses did not do well. I know that runs against the conventional wisdom that M&A's swell in bad times. But this time, the buyers stayed at home. Now, things are different."

How Not to Need a Broker

The way to avoid having to sell a business if you don't want to sell it is, of course, to avoid problems that compel you to sell it. So here are the ten main reasons why businesses fail, according to the International Business Brokers Association. All you have to do is make sure that you avoid them.

1. Insufficient profits
2. Too little, too slow growth
3. Too much debt, too little capital
4. Inexperience

5. Too much overhead
6. Industry slumps
7. Various (poor locations, competition, high interest rates)
8. Lack of interest
9. Fraud
10. Lack of planning.

part four

Financing the Merger

chapter 12

Getting Money From the Bank

Banks have had it rough. But not anymore. They've got the money to lend.

If your recent experience is anything like mine, you are being greeted by your local, friendly bank people with big smiles, refreshments, free ball-point pens and pencils and, of course, calendars. Their wide smiles are full of happy surprise, as if you weren't aware that their interest rates were near rock bottom. Rising maybe here and there but still quite low.

There are good reasons for this welcome. In the decade's first few years, American corporations were turned off on commercial banks due to the economic slump, lower interest rates and declined inflationary pressures. Instead, corporations returned to the stock and bond market to finance their short-term money needs. But now things have drastically changed. Banks are back in.

Savings institutions, too, have had a difficult time. "Credit-quality" problems dogged them. What's that? It means bad loans. It was so bad that in the first quarter of 1992, bad loans written off at Savings Association Insurance Fund-insured thrifts represented one-half percent of total assets which, while seemingly not so high, were quite high from a historical standpoint. Delinquent construction loans accounted for 12 percent of all loans in that quarter. But the situation at savings banks, too, has improved.

The tough road that commercial banks had to travel is shown in their aggregate commercial loans which dropped from $2,309 billion in 1990 to $2,288 billion in 1991 to $2,281 billion in 1992. Then they rose to $2,327 billion in 1993. In 1994, the trend was up further and was expected to round out at about $2,420 billion. The simple fact is that the banks got their act together by writing off many lingering bad loans and by divesting static or losing investments.

But the important fact is that the recovery in bank health, along with greater stability in the venture capital industry, has provided the lifeline for the vigorous trend in American mergers and acquisitions. Put another way, the sickness of the nation's financial institutions in the late 1980s and early 1990s had a depressing effect on the country's business consolidations. But that appears to be over.

A phenomenon of the merger movement of the last decade and increasingly important in the last five years has been the zeal of pension funds, endowments and foundations not only to be the dominant providers of new venture capital but to invest in business consolidations. Pension funds in particular like large investment opportunities, preferring investments in deals worth $200 million and more to those representing only 10 or 20 percent of such amounts. The most enthusiastic pension investors have been from the most populous states such as California, New York and Texas.

A Renewed Interest in Financing

Banks have been the financial mainstay of M&As, often through syndicates of banks in which one major institution has been the leading lender and others have joined to create a financing pool which has allowed merger makers to carry on their activities. In the 1980s, many consolidations were fueled by this combined effort. After a few years of slippage, the bank groups have reappeared to finance M&As, after clearing their books of poor, financial marketing judgments such as bad loans and unproductive investments.

As economic activity picked up in 1993 and 1994, American business grew more confident and turned again to commercial banks for their capital needs. Low interest rates and stable price levels also fueled more bank lending. Having stubbed their toes on investments, banks are expected to cut back on them from the peak gain of 16.5 percent in 1991 to about 10 percent in 1994 and 1995.

But deposits in commercial banks have been held to small gains by the wide variety of savings and investments instruments offered by rival depository and non-depository financial institutions. In recent years, consumers' savings deposits were adversely affected by the erosion on certificates of deposit. This was only partly countered by the increase in passbook and money market accounts. Mutual funds were the beneficiary of the shift from low-paying bank deposits and were the main stimulant in both the stock and bond markets. The relentless competition forced commercial banks to invade the mutual fund arena to provide some of its own competition. It also compelled them to keep the pressure on both regulators and legislators to allow them other competitive opportunities such as selling securities.

As a result, the Federal Reserve Board has granted approval for some banks to have broader securities underwriting powers, permitting them through separately capitalized facilities to underwrite and deal in corporate debt and equity as they already deal in government securities. But these activities can probably represent no more than 10 percent of the unit's revenues.

This has also allowed banks, however, to participate in company mergers and acquisitions in a greater variety of ways, from providing short- and long-term loans, underwriting new issues subsequent to takeovers, to acting as company finders and even owners.

Foreign banks, both in Europe and the Far East, represent about one third of the more than 30 banks which received the

Fed's approval to conduct securities underwriting under Section 20 of the Glass-Steagall Act. The rest are domestic money-center banks and large, regional banking institutions. In addition, about 17 more foreign banks have been permitted under the International Banking Act of 1978 to conduct both commercial banking and securities underwriting in the U.S.

How Banks Rate M&As and Participate in Them

Chemical Bank Corporation will not finance an unfriendly transaction on a major client of the bank but has on occasion done so when it involved a non-client, says James B. Lee, Chemical's senior managing director in charge of structured finance. In an example of non-client hostile buyouts, Chemical was the sole lender to American Product Company's successful effort to acquire American Cyanamid. "We put up $10 billion," Lee said. "But not all our participation has been on successful hostiles. We backed QVC in its abortive bid for Paramount Communications."

There are fewer hostile offers than there used to be, he said in an interview. It's become "socially distasteful." He explains, "The public's attitude has turned negative on them, in great part because the perception has been sharpened from books such as 'Barbarians at the Gates,' movies like 'Wall Street' and media coverage. The hostile has fallen out of favor almost as much as the leveraged buyout but you will still see some of both."

An 18-year veteran at Chemical and the youngest (at 41) member of the holding company's management committee, Lee describes the bank's decision to fund a merger or acquisition in broad terms. "If the customer is right, the client is right, the bank deal is right and the bond deal is right and the underlying business concept is right, the deal makes sense to us," he says.

"That's an awful lot of 'rights,' can't you be more explicit?" he was asked.

"It means that we won't do a deal that the market won't take," he replied. "The transaction has to be acceptable to us, to the market and to the client. It has to make sense credit-wise, to be a good credit risk in concept, so that we can syndicate a funding that has good credit characteristics."

He insisted that "the definition of a good deal for us to enter into is one in which all three principals are happy—the client who is the borrower or issuer, our bank and the investors in the deal which could include other banks or non-banks, particularly mutual funds."

In a $1.6 billion bank syndication in which a foreign company was making a bid for an American business, Chemical was the lead bank. Taking its own sizeable commitment, it prepared the financing allotment for the syndicate, allocating between $200 million to $300 million to mutual fund participation and the rest to be offered to the other banks, Lee said. "Mutual funds of all sorts have been interested in investing in M&As for some years now."

As head of Chemical's structured financing, Lee is responsible for loan syndication, high-yield bonds, M&As, acquisition financing and restructuring and reorganization, otherwise known as "bankruptcies." While Chemical will do a deal alone as it did for American Home Products, a vital part of defining a "good" deal is its syndication capability, it prefers a syndication arrangement in which it is the lead bank as in the case of the Forstmann Little $1 billion buyout of the Ziff-Davis Publishing Company.

Foreign acquisitions of American companies have been on the rise for the last several years, Lee says, encouraged by the dollar weakness. "I think their outlook is good as long as the U.S. dollar remains cheap relative to other currencies," he said. "Also, as European countries rebound from their recessions, they will get stronger and in the process look at the U.S. with an eye to buy companies. As to the outlook for U.S. to buy foreign businesses, I think it will depend upon whether the industry involved is of a global nature or not. If global, it would lend itself to more buyouts that cross national borders."

To what extent are American chief executives "global-minded"? "It's certainly a growing mind-set," Lee answered. "I think that we are in an age when American CEOs are preparing to advance their businesses, especially in those cases where they are questioning their opportunity to grow domestically."

Chase Manhattan Corporation, New York acts as "a facilitator and intermediary in mergers and acquisitions for the bank's clients and for key companies active in industries we focus on," observes Bernard Jacobs, senior vice president and head of the company's advisory mergers-and-acquisition practice. "We are an industry-based group in those industries where we have knowledge and expertise," he said. "We also, when requested, give advice to any clients of the bank irrespective of the industry."

As to what Chase doesn't do, he said that the bank "will stay away from small deals unrelated to our clients. But, as an overall policy, we prefer not to be involved in any situation in which we do not add value. We look for good will, not bad will. And we'll be particularly selective in participating in unfriendly transactions, especially not participating if a client of the bank is the target. One of our main goals is to help clients maximize their shareholder value."

Not all transactions begin with willing participants, he said in an interview. "So when it becomes clear that a client is the target of an unfriendly suitor, we withdraw from any participation."

The Jacobs group, numbering about 65 people worldwide, will work either on the buy or sell side. It does not get involved directly in financing but will when necessary refer that function for a client or other industry company to Chase's commercial financing side, he said. But, he added, "financing is a commodity product and we seek to operate in a dispassionate way in terms of financing needs to support our clients."

One of the current M&A trends is an increasing number of international deals, involving foreign purchases of U.S. companies and the reverse. "Cross-border transactions are on the rise primarily because of the general emphasis on global markets," Jacobs said. "It's becoming very apparent that local companies may well become global, that regional companies are global or becoming so. For many companies, such as those in the health-care and pharmaceuticals businesses, but in consumer goods companies, too, the difficulties and costs of developing new products require considerable market scope to produce the mass volume needed," he said. "The natural outlet for this is the merger-and-acquisition route. This is a fact of life not only in this country but abroad, too," Jacobs said.

As a case in point, he went on, Chase advised Grupo Synkro, a Mexican women's hosiery producer, with a 54 percent market share in its country, on how to solve its growth problem. When the Sara Lee Corporation, a diversified, American consumer goods company, entered the Mexican hosiery market, Grupo Synkro decided that it needed more volume in the market in order to compete more strongly. The Kayser Roth Corporation, maker of the "No Nonsense" hoisery brand in the U.S., was available for sale. "Our advisory functions ran the gamut," Jacobs said. "It ranged from a general advisory relationship, bringing the client the idea of acquiring Kayser Roth, evaluating it, making the first contact, following up and keeping in contact and closing the deal." The $200 million deal took about a year to complete, Jacobs said.

He is convinced that the merger trend is poised to grow in great degree because of the rapidly growing interest in the "global economy." That factor alone, he says, will bring the "next level of scope and size to the merger-acquisition business."

Banks Themselves Are Merging and Downsizing

Most observers assume that the big bank mergers are over for the 1990s but don't count on it. For one example, was there a marriage percolating between the Bank of New York, the 16th biggest bank holding company, and the Fleet Financial Group, the regional financial-services group with 850 branches throughout New England? There's strategic value for both in a merger. BNY would substantially expand its reach through acquiring all those Fleet branches as well as the big Fleet Mortgage Group. Fleet would gain a major addition to its financial services business. But Fleet decided to buy Shawmut National Bank instead.

Meanwhile, cost-cutting even at the top is noticeable among a number of banks, particularly in New York where the

Chase Manhattan Corporation, as already mentioned, is dropping 1,600 positions, and in the Boston area, too.

Having survived the economic crunch that descended upon New England beginning in the late 1980s, Boston banks are cutting back. At the Bank of Boston, three senior posts were eliminated, not to mention other layoffs. The bank's chairman, Ira Stepanian, explained that greater efficiency was needed at the pinnacle. Then, citing similar reasons, the Shawmut National Bank lopped off the job of Allen W. Sanborn, vice chairman, and two other high positions. On top of that, Joel Alvord, Shawmut's chairman, announced a cut of 600 jobs.

Does all that have any connection with the new, piercing eye that Washington plans to direct at them? Could be. The new scrutiny will come several ways. Are the big banks illegally tying bank credit extension to other services to garner a more lucrative package? Regulators will be checking into that. They will also be looking into the controversial use of derivatives as Congress weighs putting constraints on the use of these financial vehicles, already the subject of a growing number of lawsuits against commercial banks by corporate customers. In addition, the investigators will be digging into whether banks are ignoring low-earning customers, a charge that never seems to die down. Moreover, the Federal Deposit Insurance Corporation will be sending anonymous shoppers into banks to see if and what illegal marketing policies banks may be employing to entice depositors into putting money in uninsured types of investment.

It's enough to send any red-blooded banking executive into a fit of depression. It's particularly hard to take right after the banking industry has won a victory from Congress, the approval for interstate banking. On one hand they give, on the other hand—What's the problem? All banks want to do is make some money.

chapter 13

The Job Cruncher—and How You Can Ease the Crunch

Like the furious rate of mergers themselves, the uprooting effect on people has been endless and relentless:

"In (the) Takeover of Cyanamid, Shareholders Are Winners, But Workers Stand to Lose." "American Home Products is likely to cut between 2,000 and 5,000 jobs immediately and more than 10,000 total over the next two years... " (The *Wall Street Journal*, August 19, 1994.)

"Roche to Eliminate 5,000 jobs after Merger. Roche Holdings A.G., the Swiss pharmaceuticals company, said yesterday that it would cut 5,000 jobs worldwide, most of them in the United States, as part of a restructuring of its main drug division after its merger with the Syntex Corporation..." (The *New York Times*, October 18, 1994.)

"US Air will lay off about 400 of Allegheny (Commuter Airlines) employees..." (The *New York Times*, August 3, 1994).

"With the combination of Grumman (Corporation) and Northrop (Corporation), industry analysts predicted that 10 to 12 percent of their total work force, which will be more than 40,000 people, will be laid off..." (The *New York Times*, April 5, 1994).

187

As it prepares to be formally acquired by Federated Department Stores, "(R.H.) Macy is expected to dismiss about a third of its 300 administrative employees at its Manhattan corporate headquarters later this week..." (The *New York Times*, August 16, 1994).

On and on it goes. As businesses marry, employees are let go either in big or little bites. The major cause is, of course, redundancy. Why, if two similar companies merge, should they retain two separate controllers, two accountants, marketing directors, their assistants and so on? Especially since from the nuptial moment the emphasis is on cutting costs so that the debt incurred is paid off as quickly as possible. In a broad sense, it's reminiscent of the old adage that "two can live as cheaply as one," but it doesn't, of course, work that way. If two companies become one, it's hardly likely that their cost will be tantamount to one. Economy of scale, the great American rationale for giantism, seeks to establish that bigness provides economies through enhanced efficiency. But what it ignores is that economy of scale does carry a higher expense factor since the burden of critical mass is that it does cost more.

Are Fewer Really Better?

The proof, of course, is in the performance. But so ingrained into the country's marrow is the acceptance of business mergers and downsizing that most professionals and laymen directly or indirectly involved in merger-prone industries accept the claim that fewer employees, given more enlightened supervision, can produce more.

But if almost 30 percent of all mergers fail, is letting so many people go nothing but waste? Is it unreality plus expediency chasing frustration? Or simply the traditional *modus operandi* for business to cut heads as one of its first and patently easiest strategic moves in order to cut expenses? In any case, it's a big question not about to be answered without a major research study involving months and years of effort, if even then.

Coincident with the people crunch wrought by M&As is the widespread downsizing that American corporations have undertaken in the recent recession. But is that also an expedient used by senior managers to ignore the lack of management expertise that might have converted the downsizing concept to one of more productive strategic realignment? In fact, the human cutbacks due to downsizing moves have been so pervasive that they probably have submerged and mitigated the true degree and damage of people displacement due to mergers and acquisitions.

Because of that mix of cutbacks and layoffs, it's difficult to get pure numbers for the M&A-caused dislocations. It's in the many thousands. And don't count on it to be included in the jobless rate which is largely based on those seeking unemployment benefits. Lots of senior- and middle-management executives terminated by mergers do not seek those benefits out of pride or actual absence of need. But their income-earning careers have definitely been interrupted, perhaps ended.

Excepting monthly and quarterly changes, the American employment trend has not been a strong one, as civilian population grew but employment remained static and the jobless rate rose. In 1992, generally considered the jump-off point for the country's economic turnaround, the total population was about 257 million, of which the labor force consisted of 128.5 million. Of that total, 117.6 million were employed in civilian jobs, but about 9.3 million were unemployed. The year's 7.3 percent jobless rate was the highest since 1984's 7.4 percent. It was not a crunch year but from a labor standpoint it was not a good year. Too many were unemployed.

In the subsequent two years, the employment numbers have gone up and the jobless rate has been whittled down. But the 6 percent unemployment rate remains higher than that of the later 1980s or those of 1950 and 1960. What these trends say is that there are many employable people in the approximate 9 million out of jobs. This should be challenging American business to be creative in developing opportunities both for them and for itself.

Workers Are Making An Impact

In July 1994, the shareholders of UAL Corporation, the parent of United Airlines, approved the award of 55 percent of company stock to several employee groups in exchange for $4.9 billion worth of wage and productivity concessions and givebacks. Although United Airlines is now America's largest employee-owned company, as mentioned earlier, fighting among the employee groups, a pilots' strike, threats by well-known raiders and other pesky matters will make the employee ownership difficult and hazardous. UAL employees won four seats on the company board and succeeded in replacing management with a choice of their own, Gerald Greenwald, the former vice chairman of Chrysler Corporation. And they also won contractual agreements preventing management from laying off workers or disposing of assets that would eliminate any more jobs.

It was the fourth attempt by the employees to carve out an important ownership stake in the company—and if it doesn't succeed it might well be the last. UAL has lost many millions of dollars in the last three years, $1 billion in 1992 alone. It could eke out a profit by 1995, quite possibly from the reduced labor costs contained in the new contract with employees. Besides its internal problems, the airline is fighting the competition's hard-driving cut-price offers, short-haul fights and heavy advertising and promotion.

In the meantime, the employee control of one of America's biggest airlines is being hailed as something new on the American labor-management horizon—an intelligent substitute for the job-crunching machine set loose by cost-battered companies. "If United is successful, this will be a major landmark in American business history," declared Robert Reich, U.S. Secretary of Labor, when the shareholders put the employees in the pilot's seat.

A similar but much smaller transaction involving employee ownership occurred only two months later in the steel industry. Joined by a New York investment group, the United Steelworkers bought two closed plants which had been operated by the Bethlehem Steel Corporation until 1992. The USW agreed to flexible work rules and lower pay scales more typical of small mill operations than of large mills. For that, the union got 800 new jobs, a 25 percent equity and two seats on the board of directors at the new company, known as BRW Steel Corporation. The real target wasn't to uproot or unseat management but to combat non-union "mini-mills" which have stolen jobs and market share because of the labor-cost difference.

Will it work? The BRW deal will allow the union to put new muscle into its organizing efforts at the non-union mini-mills, brandishing the "equity" carrot. But it could also work against the union's future negotiations with major steel companies who could insist on concessions similar to those it gave BRW.

But there's another way in which employees can take a stand on business mergers, particularly if they do not like the terms. Late in 1994, the pension fund of the International Brotherhood of Teamsters said it would not approve the contemplated takeover of Borden Inc. by Kohlberg, Kravis & Roberts. The $46 billion pension fund said that the offered share value of $14.25 was not enough and so the fund declined to sell its 247,000 shares of Borden to KKR. In the deal, the investment banker planned to exchange $2 billion of its RJR Nabisco stock for Borden common.

In the fund's statement of the decision, William B. Patterson, the fund's director, asserted, "We will be telling stockholders that we believe that there is greater value to be attained by hanging on to the shares and realizing the full potential of the Borden name. Borden shareholders are getting their stock purchased when it's at rock bottom when it has upside possibilities," he said.

Not quite the same as running a company, for sure, but it could be effective in another, meaningful way to pressure a recalcitrant management or attacker. Except that in the case of Borden, it didn't work. As 1994 ended, Kohlberg, Kravis & Roberts announced that it had won control of Borden since 63.5 percent of its shareholders had accepted the tender offer. But because RJR's stock had slipped, KKR had to shave its offer of $14.25 a share to $13.32 a share. It was a bitter pill for the Teamsters as well as for other investors to swallow.

What to Do If You Lose Your Job in a Merger

The worst thing to do if you should be terminated due to a merger or acquisition is to take a vacation, just play golf, or sit back and brood on your situation and wait for the telephone to ring. Executive recruiters and outplacement experts say that the best therapy for people in a suddenly displaced role is to keep busy and make a job out of getting a job. "It's basically shoe-leather time," says Herbert Mines, one of New York's busiest executive recruiters, "for eight hours a day. It produce results and it keeps you from brooding."

Robert Nesbit, managing partner of Korn/Ferry International, the nation's biggest recruiting firm, asserts, "You should shout from the rooftops that you are available for a new position. Never, never go into seclusion. Never assume that everyone knows that you are available. You just can't rely on that. Finding a new job should become the most demanding job that you have ever had. Surprisingly, marketing people seem to find it the hardest to switch from selling a product or service to selling themselves."

Here's a list of additional suggestions from these two top recruiters and others:

- Prepare a very good resume and "paper the world with it."

- Communicate with every contact you have made up till now. Call suppliers, vendors, wholesalers, consultants, or anyone you had business with. "Don't worry about making a pest of yourself by calling often," Nesbit says. "Your last call can be the one that pays off." He tells of an executive who kept calling him frequently to find if anything appropriate was available. Finally, the job-seeker made yet another call just after Nesbit had hung up on an employer looking for the very type of experience that the applicant had. Because of the timing, the applicant got the job.

- Be patient as well as persistent. How long does it usually take for a male or female senior or middle executive caught in the job crunch to find a new one? Usually, between a year and 18 months. Those with a high job profile (reputation) often can do it in much less time.

- Be flexible on salary. There's usually a 20 to 30 percent earnings dilution between the previous job and the new one. "You have to accept it or else stay on the beach," Nesbit says. "So, it's either X dollars minus 20 or 30 percent or no dollars at all."

- Review your personal finances so that you know what you have and what you need. "We tell them to sit down with their spouses and go over their financial status and responsibilities," said Herbert Mines. "It clears the air for the job seeker, spouse, and their family."

Getting a Job Is All a Matter of Attitude

The people crunch created by mergers and acquisitions is at its highest level in the memory of executive recruiters, with an unusually high number of senior executives cast out along with many middle-rank people. These people are "distressed, they feel unworthy because while they thought they were productive they evidently weren't and they feel betrayed by the system," is how the recruiters describe them.

And so the recruiters take pains to explain to them that they aren't alone in feeling that way and that there will be more and more laid-off executives. Many of the senior executives were earning at least $150,000 but their ability to obtain jobs with at least that salary often depends upon their age. It's sensitive at 50, difficult at 55 and almost impossible at 60 or above, the recruiters say.

"Everything else being equal or reasonable, a man or woman in career transit absolutely has to maintain self-confidence," says Robert Nesbit, "or no one else will. If these people feel impelled to ask themselves, 'did I fail my employer?' or 'will I always be identified as a loser?' they have to say no to each."

Many senior executives are lulled into a sense of security and physical lassitude by the large severage packages they get, often ranging between $600,000 and $900,000, when a merger is consummated with their companies, observes Joseph

Carideo, partner at Thorndike Deland Associates, one of New York's oldest executive recruiters. "They figure that they can sit back, be very choosy with any offers they get and trust that something good will develop for them while they enjoy the comfort of the big lump sum," says Carideo. "But it just does-n't work that way. 'If you are out of the active scene for 12 to 18 months, you've become dusty,' I tell them, 'and you need to become reinvolved very soon after you leave the old employer. You've got to look hungry even if you have that great cash cushion, which, by the way, won't last as long as you think.'"

But how? By being "pro-active." That means going out to prospective employers, calling suppliers and keeping after the head-hunters, Carideo says. Taking on projects as a consultant is a worthwhile interim step, he adds, because it reaffirms one's reputation for expertise. But, above all, he insists, don't be like the top executive who refused to go to an interview with a company in voluntary bankruptcy. "Why should I respond to the first interview I get and especially with that company?" he told Carideo. But when the recruiter urged him to go because of the exposure, the man went and was inter-viewed by several of the company's creditors. Bottom-line: he didn't get the job with the bankrupt company but one of the creditors he spoke to was impressed and recommended him for an opening at another company. "He got that job," Carideo said. "And it was closer in salary and position to the job he had lost."

Another case but with a different ending concerned a well-known executive, one with a "marquee" name. He was a charis-matic, 51-year-old man with considerable experience who wanted to get back into harness after a long, leisurely layoff. But after an interview with a number of people at a large com-pany, he returned to the search firm and was told that he did-n't get the job. "They said that you weren't animated enough," he was told. "They didn't think you were hungry enough for the job." Added Carideo, "In other words, they were looking for the substance behind the demeanor and didn't find enough of it."

Then there are the high-profile, top executives well-known in industry who immediately begin receiving calls from prospective employers once the word gets out that they are available. Such people generally are "snapped up," as one recruiter put it, within 60 to 90 days after being on the loose. Most of the others not in that fortunate position are confused, lost and generally at sea and need guidance from experienced recruiters or outplacement specialists.

But almost all displaced executives are shocked by the sudden reality of being out on the street after having worked long for a company. "They need a lot of hand-holding," says Herbert Mines, "because essentially they are on their own even if their former employer has its own outplacement service. But after two or three weeks, they get themselves in order. It may take them a year or more to get relocated. That's a long time to keep your spirits up. But it's essential that they do. Of course, they can buy a franchise or open a small store of some kind. Many of them do just that."

So, next time you are in a 7-Eleven, a Domino's Pizza, a Wendy's or MacDonald's or some other fast-food restaurant, don't be too surprised if the man serving you is a former corporate executive.

In the meantime—expect more layoffs.

Are the Jobless Numbers Right?

For some time now, I have personally been puzzled by the gap between the low unemployment rates that the Federal government reports every month and my own perception of how many people are unemployed as I see them or hear about them. My sense is that since the government bases its data on those men and women filing for unemployment benefits, it may be overlooking those who aren't working and aren't reporting anymore for benefits.

Therefore, I was intrigued by *Business Week*'s article in its November 7, 1994 issue claiming that many of the government's economic statistics are wrong. In particular, the magazine cited the unemployment rate as too low, the inflation rate as too high, and the business equipment report as fully 30 percent understated.

In terms of the unemployment rate, the magazine stated:

"A true picture of the economy would also show that Americans are right to be worried about jobs these days, despite the low unofficial unemployment rate. Increasingly, the labor market is filled with surplus workers who are not being counted as unemployed. The rate of labor force participation—those working or looking for work—has dropped sharply for men since 1989. Estimated conservatively, some 1.1 million more prime-age male workers are out of the labor force compared with five years ago. Adding those workers back in would push the real unemployment rate to 6.8 percent, from its reported 5.9 percent. And there are at least 500,000 more workers with some college who have jobs but are underemployed compared to 5 years ago. That's an enormous pool of surplus labor available to fuel the economy's growth."

There's much to think about here. White-collar or blue-collar, there are many surplus workers in the U.S., whether as a result of mergers, company downsizing or an up-and-down economy, contributing precious little to American productivity largely not because of their own doing. To the extent that mergers and acquisitions add to it, the problem should give pause to government, corporate officials and local politicians. If too many mergers fail, isn't it just as likely that many layoffs or terminations caused by them do not work, either? And what does that say about waste of a very precious commodity?

chapter 14

Busy Days for Minideals

Imagine Gatorade and Snapple together. A new, multiple delight for the Adam's apple: one, the thirst-quenching remedy for perspiring half-backs and quarterbacks; the other, the sipping joy of young professionals. They were oddly coupled in an acquisition that dramatized how well a small company can do as it rides the crest of the 1990s merger tide.

In November 1994, when Quaker Oats Company announced a transaction to buy the Snapple Beverage Corporation for $1.7 billion, the price seemed enormous. The 22-year old company, launched in Brooklyn, first produced all-natural fruit drinks for health-food stores and then broadened its products to include iced teas, all-natural beverages and seltzers for the general trade. Sales rose to $700 million as the company, relocated to Long Island, generated a marketing drive across the country to the West Coast. Quaker Oats, which had acquired Gatorade in 1983 in a merger with Stokley-Van Camp and built it to its biggest product in sales, was willing to shell out an excellent price to create the third-largest beverage company in the U.S.

But the event didn't conclude at just that point. Simultaneous with the acquisition announcement, Snapple took the occasion to disclose that its third-quarter income had plummeted 74 percent and that sales had fallen 6 percent from the prior-year level. While that may have prompted Quaker Oats to pull back a bit with its $14-per-share cash offer, it didn't. Snapple shareholders were angry. They had seen their shares slip from a 1994 high of $32.25 to a current value of about $12. It was not quite the happy day that the founders of Snapple and its president and chief executive, Leonard Marsh, had envisioned. Both he and the Quaker Oats' chairman, William D. Smithberg, spoke enthusiastically of the prospects for the combined company. But the glow had faded from the process—smaller company makes good, is acquired, gets excellent price but its investors howl. It was not typical of mergers and acquisitions of smaller- and medium-sized companies.

One Busy Day in Minideals

On August 25, 1994 alone, there were five mergers or acquisitions reported in the national media. Each was smaller in value than almost all the major transactions we've mentioned so far. Such minideals far outnumber the megadeals. And there are many more even smaller ones that never see the light of day in print, are transacted quietly and become part of the everyday fabric of American business.

But they are interesting in their own right and demonstrate that the motivation of small company or divisional M&As is strategically similar to those of the larger deals. The thrust to grow and expand among small- and medium-sized companies, however, is complicated by their ever-rising cost of operations, not the least of which is created by the need to comply with government regulations, whether federal, state or local. Compared to the big companies, the ratio of cost-to-sales among the smaller companies is becoming enormous and disproportionate. As a result, mergers can also provide a financial lifeline, sacrificing independence for economic security.

On that August day, Xerox Corporation, the Stamford, Connecticut copier company, agreed to sell its Xerox Financial Services Life Insurance Company to the General American Life Insurance Company, St. Louis, for an undisclosed amount.

Why? Well, Xerox had been diversifying but its management reversed this policy and had begun divesting financial services units to concentrate on its copier business. For its part, General American elected to raise its assets 50 percent by buying the Xerox unit, expanding its core of fixed and variable financial products. So with one company divesting and the other adding, it was like two friendly ships stopping to exchange stores instead of just passing in the night.

In another transaction that day, the Dole Food Company, the fruit and juice producer, made a bid to acquire the remaining 17 percent stake that it didn't already have in Castle & Cooke Homes Inc., the real-estate developer, at a cost of about $72 million.

Why? The Los Angeles-based Castle & Cooke was aggressively building single-family homes on the island of Oahu in Hawaii where Dole has its principal operations. Having considerable land in the Hawaiian Islands, lots of employees and a deep proprietary feeling about its presence there, Dole now wanted all of Castle & Cooke, which also was building homes in such other hot-weather states as California and Arizona.

Regina Company, an Atlanta-based, old-line maker of vacuum cleaners and floor care products, signed an agreement to be acquired by Pass-Port Ltd., a diversified company in Tel Aviv, Israel, for an amount to be disclosed later. Why? Regina's private investors saw investment growth in a busy, foreign acquirer which had previously purchased Health Science Properties of California, a real-estate company, and 281 condominiums in New York. Pass-Port was banking on the eventual boom in both commercial and residential real-estate and its stimulus on home-care products.

In another hands-across-the-seas deal that day, the Westinghouse Electric Company was reported to be in talks to sell at least part of its 75 percent of Westinghouse Motor Company to Teco Electric and Machinery, a Taiwanese company which was a minority holder in Westinghouse Motor. Why?

The company being sold had been founded in 1988 as a joint venture between Westinghouse and Teco. Now Teco wanted to own additional equity to give it more control of operations while Westinghouse reportedly was interested in cashing in some of its stake. Another case of two different motivations meshing to arrange an accommodation for each company.

The fifth transaction that day was a simple, straight-line case of one bank holding company buying another to increase market share in the state of Michigan. The Old Kent Financial Corporation, based in Grand Rapids, Michigan, said it would buy First National Bank Corporation, Mount Clemens, Michigan, for $92.9 million. Old Kent already had 16 affiliate banks with 221 offices in Michigan and Illinois and assets of $10.4 billion and by early 1995, when the deal would be consummated, it would also have First National's 16 offices in the northeastern suburbs of Detroit. Why? Market growth for the Old Kent bank stable and more security for the smaller bank company.

Examining the Minideal Strategy

No big deals, any of them? Maybe not. In each of them, though, there's a strategy at work for both buyer and seller. There's no swooping up of assets of one company by another just for self-aggrandizement. Of course, implicitly every time one company tells another it wants to buy it or part of it, the target company turns on a defensive posture. Then it becomes a question of resisting or accommodating at the right price.

In fact, the churning among smaller companies is much more intense than it is among the big players, partly because there are so many of the former and the pressures of survival are so much greater. The traditional reluctance to tie up with or be bought out by a larger company has diminished in the interest of participating in a greater, entrepreneurial opportunity or greater financial resources.

Otherwise, why would, say, a specialty brewer in Seattle, the Redhook Ale Brewery Inc., agree to enter into a distribution and equity deal with the world's biggest brewer, the Anheuser-

Busch Companies, as it did recently? Redhook produces five brands of European-style ale and over its 12-year history was able to develop a good demand in the Pacific Northwest among consumers who liked that type of brew. Anheuser-Busch, seeking to add one more niche to its broad market exposure, offered to take a minority position in Redhook and distribute its brand outside the Northwest. On the surface, at least, a mutually advantageous arrangement.

How to "Go Public" Without Going Public

Suppose your small- to medium-sized company wants to go public without the hassle and expense of actually offering your company's stock in a public issue? There's a way.

For 40 years, Audits & Surveys Worldwide, a New York-based marketing research company, grew under the paternal but watchful eye of Sol Dutka, the founder and chief executive officer, adding an average $1 million revenues each year. In this process, it became one of the largest American research companies.

As American demographics became more complex requiring sophisticated networking and thorough databases, the company opened a 100-person office in Portland, Oregon, giving it eight domestic and four foreign offices. The reporting network also served to offset the time differential that could have complicated efficient operations.

In August 1994, Audits & Surveys merged with Triangle Corporation, a metal goods fabricator in Stamford, Connecticut, which had previously sold its hand tools, horseshoes and horseshoe-tools business. In effect, A&S was acquiring 80 percent of the public stock of Triangle. It was a surprising move for a stable, closely held company. Why? Dutka was asked.

"Actually, it was something that I thought I would never do," he said in an interview. "Why should a group of professionals become a public company? But we realized that there are certain realities which you can deal with without compromising your professional standards."

For many years, A&S was a Sub-Chapter S company, which under Internal Revenue Service regulations permits a company with a limited number of shareholders to divide all its profits among them and thus avoid paying a double tax. The corporation need not pay federal income taxes because it has no profit at year-end and its shareholders need only pay personal income taxes. But, as Dutka pointed out, "The downside of it is that since the company retains no earned income, it also has no reserve."

He explained that a company may distribute dividends "but it also needs reserves to underwrite new products, support its growth plan, modernize equipment and make acquisitions. We were able to expand and 'grow' the company out of current earnings. That's fine but pursuing that course you would eventually run out of cash."

Seeking to avoid that cash erosion, A&S would reborrow the distributed profits from its shareholders, use the funds and pay the interest on it. "We've been following this scenario for some time," said Dutka. "But a new reality entered the situation. A number of my executives had been with me for some time, were getting older and wanted to retire. We had a buyout program to take care of that. But the publicly held information companies had an excellent price/earnings multiple by comparison of between 20 and 30 times earnings."

One way out was for A&S to go public. But it elected not to, Dutka says, because "the public underwriting often takes you to the brink and then the underwriter or the bank says 'the market isn't ready.' Meantime, the lawyers and the accountants have cost you a lot and there you are no better off than before. So, we bought a 'shell' company, a public company with few if any assets, which cost less than an initial public offering, and we spring forth like Athena fully listed on the American Stock Exchange."

With that move, A&S's executives have a marketable stock and the company has the wherewithal to make acquisitions and also to distribute stock options. Later, the company will make a secondary offering to capitalize on its public status, says Dutka. Triangle will change its name to that of Audits & Surveys Worldwide, the combined company to be based in New York.

More Reasons for Selling Out

But there are other reasons why smaller firms merge or buy each other out. Some do it for surprising reasons, others for convenience. Let's examine a few examples.

- The company didn't have a new president so it bought a company that did. Yes, that does happen. This is particularly true in the retailing, apparel and textile industries where a company can rise or fall on the merits and charisma of its chief executive, chief merchant or sales vice president. In fact, lots of companies in those fields keep a constant check on competitors' people whose personality or personal contacts give him or her an edge. Recently, a company run by an aging founder engaged an investment banker to find a firm which could provide an outstanding successor if it were acquired. The banker did so. But wouldn't it have been cheaper, less traumatic and more efficient just to hire the guy away? Of course. But there was only one problem. The hotshot was the owner of his company. If you wanted him, you had to take his company, too.

- They couldn't compete with the company, so they bought it. This happens more often than many people think. In one case that I know, a truck-hauling company was losing serious ground to a rival which had newer, bigger trucks, more modern warehouses and a more sophisticated communications system. The weaker company's accountant quipped one day, "Why don't you guys buy him out? It would be cheaper in the long run than trying to replicate all his equipment." The owner thought about it and did just that. In another case, the buyout was even simpler and more direct. A weaker company just went out and bought its stronger competitor. What? You're waiting for the kicker, that either or both those transactions didn't work? Wrong. They both did, the last I heard.

- The company really didn't want to sell; it just wanted to see what kind of price it could draw. Well, I'm sure you are way ahead of me on that one. Life is just full of surprises. After letting the word out that it might be available, the company I am referring to was so pleasantly surprised at the high price it drew that it actually considered selling but finally said no. However, the toothsome bait had been dangled. Months later, the company was sold. Now, I grant you that that's not quite the whole story. There were other factors, some of which I do not know. There might have been serious illness at the top or just fatigue or malaise. But, then again, if it hadn't waved that "for sale" flag, the sale probably wouldn't have happened.

- This is the strangest of all—The company really didn't want to buy any other companies but just couldn't resist it. It just loved the exercise and excitement of it. I am reminded of two business owners in particular who sincerely believed that the only way to run a company was to buy another company and use the original firm as collateral. Then it would buy another the same way and so on, building a structure in which the latest acquisition was shakily supported by the earlier ones. Of course, this kind of idiocy couldn't last. In the one case, the company toppled from the inertia that set in from the poorly-matching acquisitions and filed for bankruptcy. In the other case, the owner died suddenly, leaving a corporate mess that still remains unsettled.

- "Don't leave your money in the bank—use it or lose it." This was actually told to me by one of the most active acquirers I know. What he meant related, of course, to the logic of the cases just forementioned. Banks pay as little interest as they can get away with, he meant, while stocks and bonds pay better. But buying and selling companies pays best, likewise investing in them. Well, I'd like to say that his philosophy bombed. But it didn't and "Mr. Use It or Lose It" is still running wild.

So there's the boom in small-company mergers and the reasons for many of them. If some of those reasons disturb you because they make little sense, you're forgetting one small fact of life. Big companies can't take flyers. They've got too many employees, shareholders, investors and creditors whose rights must be protected or who will complain bitterly if they aren't. But small companies have fewer strings and are more free to take a fling. And they do, too. But the more surprising thing is that most spurn the concept of a strategic combination. Maybe that's why so many stay small.

chapter 15

The Future—More, and Big and Bigger

SmithKline Beecham Sterling-Winthrop Merck Bristol Colgate Procter & Gamble Corporation?

In September 1994, the British company of SmithKline Beecham announced the $2.9 billion purchase of Eastman Kodak's Sterling-Winthrop's over-the-counter pharmaceuticals business. It was SmithKline's second, multibillion purchase in a four-month period, the latest acquisition in a proliferating international business empire.

Is the mega-mouthful above the future of American and global business? It brings to mind the SmithKline full-page advertisement in the Sunday *New York Times*, proclaiming, "Now we are one" in noting its then latest takeover. Was it only the first of an annual declaration of acquisitive pride or just a momentary outburst? For a valid answer, we'll have to wait for SmithKline's next takeover. But it's reasonable to expect more.

Will the continuous joining, molting, cross-market inter-twining of major American and foreign corporations become so cumbersome that, like the big advertising agencies, the combinations will have to be addressed by a string of letters. For example, would the hypothetical SmithKline one above have to be called SKBMBCP&G? Or, like the New York-area electronics retailer which has legalized its name into a full sentence, "Nobody Beats the Wiz," will the drugs combination simply be called "Absolutely Nobody Is Bigger than SKBMBCP&G"?

Facetiousness aside, the merger-acquisition wave of the 1990s, the second biggest in recent history, has been dominated by three main characteristics: size, number of transactions, and strategic motivations. On the negative side, the three elements have combined to further concentrate American business into fewer hands, diminish competition in industries and regional markets, at least temporarily hurt local economies and throw many thousands of people out of work. On the positive side, they have taken the slack and fat out of many companies, turned the combined organizations into more efficiently operating entities, prompted competitors to become defensively more efficient and held out the promise that they will eventually benefit the local economies.

Even if one were to assume that the negative were outweighed by the positive, two elements remained ignored by that assumption. One is the matter of the dislocated employees, the often forgotten piece in the picture. What will happen to them? Can they be retrained? If retrained, will there be jobs for them? How many are too old and effectively untrainable? And, at the core, what adverse effect on the U.S. economy will come from having hundreds of thousands of terminated employees scrambling to stay alive economically?

The second element ignored by the tradeoff in mergers is the fact that many mergers do not succeed. Among diversified mergers, to repeat, the most frequent estimate of non-successes is about 70 percent. Among strategically-based mergers, the figure is much lower, estimated at about 30 percent. It is a solemn fact, mentioned a number of times in the foregoing pages, that many mergers and acquisitions, including those strategically-motivated, are ill-conceived. They suffer from lack of sufficient research, poor due diligence, ego gratification as opposed to strategic fit, greediness on the part of the professionals who serve either the buying or selling side, and woefully bad human relations.

Is this damning the general concept by concentrating on specific difficulties? No, that is not intended. But it's the exceptions that should raise questions about rampant tendencies in an economic trend that is so important that it is carving major, permanent swaths in American industry. Too many top executives believe that buying someone else's business is the panacea to their problems. They are little concerned about their shareholders. They run away from the transaction once it's completed. And they show little consideration toward the staffs of acquired companies. All this has been compounded by a general lack of Federal oversight for the last 18 years, although that has improved somewhat in the first two years of the Clinton administration. But in general, the animal has been allowed to run free and wild.

The Matter of Size: Big and Ever Bigger?

What's a big merger? Any deal with a value of $1 billion is certainly one of major dimensions but most professional merger people consider one worth $3 billion an authentically big one. And there have been lots of them.

From July 25 through October 5, 1994, or in about 70 days, as the *New York Times* noted in its issue of November 3, 1994, there have been 10 with a value greater than $10 billion. The smallest, with the most recent bid at $3.5 billion, was Union Pacific Corporation's hostile tender offer for the Santa Fe Pacific Corporation. Seven mergers were worth more than $5 billion. Two were valued at $13 billion or more. Bell Atlantic Company's cellular phone division offered $13 billion for Nynex Company's cellular phone business. And Airtouch Communications Corporation's cellular phone business bid $13.5 billion for U.S. West Company's cellular phone company.

A little analysis of that "big ten" might be in order. Two deals, which happened to be the two largest, were carried out in a pooling of assets into a new joint venture. Five were friendly in nature. Four of those involved an exchange of stock. The fifth was a cash tender offer. One was an outright cash purchase of a divested business unit. Two were hostile bids. Most deals are friendly.

About 20 percent (probably an unusually high percentage in this case) were hostile. The bigger the company's assets and equipment, the higher the purchase price. Most deals (typical of the 1990s variety) were stock for stock. In this group instance, both hostile bidders won their targets after sweetening their offers. The most common broad-based industry involved was health-care and pharmaceuticals, totalling four transactions. The next most common was telecommunications, with three deals. The single ones included aircraft, consumer products and railroads.

How typical is this 10-deal microcosm? After all, it was only a fraction of a fraction of the 4,000 to 4,500 M&As estimated for 1994. But, in most aspects, the lineup of deals was typical. Most bigger transactions are in the health-care and pharmaceuticals fields. Telecommunications are second. Most M&As involve a stock exchange. Hostile bidders usually do win out but only after they raise their offering prices.

But what is most striking about the "big ten" reported by the *Times* (with Securities Data Company as the source) is that they were all "big" deals if one can accept the common definition of "big." The fact is that since the merger boom began reverberating in 1993 after two slow years, there have been more big deals than ever before. The 1988 RJR Nabisco three-way battle involved a price tag of $30 billion. But the abortive 1994 merger between Bell Atlantic and Tele-Communications Inc. had the higher ante of $33 billion. Why did it fall apart? "It came unglued for several reasons but primarily because of fear over cable regulation which would ultimately have limited the combined company's potential," opines Steven Wolitzer, co-head of Lehman Brothers mergers-and-acquisition practice. "Also, I think that the senior managements of both companies realized that they had vastly different cultures. The withdrawal, from what I can gather, was pretty much mutual."

How likely are more big deals and especially megadeals? Wolitzer was asked.

"We certainly see a lot of $1 billion-plus deals," he replied, "but over $5 billion and $10 billion I suspect will be rare. In other words, I don't think we will see many more deals on the order of the Martin Marietta $5.2 billion takeover of Lockheed Corporation or the $9.27 billion deal by American Home

Products to acquire American Cyanamid. But no one I know is saying 'never.' I could envision, say, if two Bell companies merge, like Nynex and US West, that could be a $30 billion-plus deal. Will they or others like them get together? Who can tell?"

"Who can tell?" indeed. The fact is that both the initial RJR Nabisco and the Bell Atlantic-TCI merger announcements came as stunning surprises to outsiders. And, based on a number of factors already presented in this book—the great vitality of strategic mergers, the global thrust that is so stimulating to both American and foreign companies, and the increasing availability of financing from banks, investment bankers, pension and mutual funds—more megadeals are definitely augured for the next few years and beyond. In fact, the awesome $30 billion deals may well be outstripped by $40 billion, $50 billion and even $60 billion transactions in global tie-ups that transcend not only oceans but past and present norms.

"Who can tell?" (to use Steve Wolitzer's expression) if an international consolidation might see Sony Corporation of Japan merging with the Siemens' electronic giant of Germany? Or General Motors merging with Toyota Motors? Or AT&T tying up with Phillips Electronics of the Netherlands? Or Wal-Mart Stores, America's biggest retail chain, buying or being bought by Japan's premier retailer Daiei Inc.? Or, in the U.S., say, a marriage of the two largest private corporations, Cargill and Koch Industries, in a glorious splash of wheat, cattle feed and oil?

All those, of course, would be mergers of great scope. But I'll bet even at this moment, there are some investment or commercial bankers on either side of the Atlantic or Pacific oceans eagerly toying with databases with such massive projects in mind, and hardly dismayed by the astronomical numbers involved.

Considering the Number of M&As: Steady or Unlimited?

In speculating about the future numbers of M&As, I would say steady, yes; unlimited, maybe. Does this seem fantastic? Not really. Let me offer some kernels for thought so that you can arrive at your own conclusions. Implicit in these tidbits are chunks of dynamism that aren't easily shrugged off:

- Continental Cablevision Corporation agreed for $1.4 billion in a stock exchange to buy the cable systems of the Providence Journal. Continental is the third-largest cable company, with 3.1 million subscribers. The Journal's systems, which have 750,000 subscribers, include such networks as Colony Communications, Copley/Colony and King Videocable. The transaction will transform Continental from a private to a public company but its main objective is strategic. In an era of stiffening competition by size, the smaller or mid-sized cable companies can hardly compete with the accumulating giants which are actually becoming industry conglomerates. Systems with 750,000 to 1.5 million subscribers simply can only struggle. And larger but not first-rank cable companies such as Continental must expand in order to slug it out with the top rank.

  As a result, cable industry experts expect the top 20 companies to engage in a wholesale marriage ceremony over time so that eventually there will be only four or five majors left. That means at least five to 10 transactions to come. But that's only one dimension of the Continental-Journal deal. By divesting its cable operations, the Providence, Rhode Island, newspaper company hopes to expand its newspaper, television and video programming entities. That means a separate round of mergers or acquisitions. The point, aside from the structural churning under way in the cable television business, is that mergers, acquisitions or divestitures have more than one side. The result is a flurry of consolidations which in turn can lead to others, ripples creating more ripples.

- In another example of proliferating technology driving the merger-acquisition trend, Microsoft Corporation, the largest software producer, offered $1.5 billion in a stock exchange to merge with Intuit Inc., which produces Quicken, the software industry's leader in personal finance. As part of that deal, Microsoft agreed to sell Money, a competitive software to Quicken, to Novell Inc. But to acquire Intuit, Microsoft paid heavily to the extent of 60 times Intuit earnings, to make the deal. The move showed how anxious Microsoft is to strike a big stake into electronic banking as a companion to its massive one in computer software. That goal was further demonstrated when Microsoft completed an arrangement to provide software for electronic shopping with Visa International.

The point here is that technological leaders tend to want to expand into other niches of technology, even when it means crossing over into new disciplines or thresholds. If for no other reason, there will be a continuing spate of big and small takeovers as a result of this demand to extend technological and market reach. But there could be hitches, of course, as in any negotiations, especially over the value of the transaction.

As a friend told me proudly, "My son has this computer business down near Atlanta. General Electric keeps calling him to buy his company. He wants $16 million. But they have only offered $12 million. He told them he's holding out for his price. But they said that there are many small development companies out there like his so they'll only hold the offer open for a short time. He's really in a tizzy."

- If recent transactions are a reliable barometer, foreign acquisitions of American companies will grow steadily. A good example is that of Ciba-Geigy Ltd., Basel, Switzerland, a large, biotechnology company, which bought a 49.9 percent interest in Chiron Corporation, the second-largest, independent, American biotechnology firm, for $2.1 billion. The transaction is complex with Ciba-Geigy buying 11.9 million shares of Chiron's common stock for $117 a share while Chiron would issue the Swiss buyer 6.6 million new shares for its international diagnostics business and a 50 percent interest in another company.

  The investment's benefits were mutual. Ciba-Geigy would acquire a funnel for future products and Chiron would receive technical, financial and service resources. The Swiss company, which had been a Chiron investor since 1983 when Chiron became a public company, would also be able to buy more shares to give it an eventual 55 percent interest in Chiron after five years.

But there were other benefits, too. With the financial infusion, Chiron said it planned to look at other firms or technologies for possible acquisitions. Those ripples again. The Ciba-Geigy and Chiron deal was only one of many already consummated and of many to come later. As the European Common Market takes hold and economies begin to prosper—a cause-and-effect equation already working—the European companies will want to expand by acquiring foreign companies. The same can be expected from the new North American Free Trade Agreement involving Mexico, Canada and the United States.

Of course, the ripples will flow the other way, too. As American companies see European and Latin American markets thrive and foreign companies gain from it, they will want to acquire in those areas too. This two-way company auction is already well under way but should gain perceptibly in the next few years with a resulting rise in the number of transactions. And Asia, the Mid- and Far East will not be far behind.

I have tried not to mention the word "global" again. But it will be one of the most pervasive reasons for business consolidations anywhere, in the major developed countries first and the less developed next.

Strategy: Stretching Strength to the Maximum

If there's a single, saving grace to the M&A binge, it must be that a good many transactions are for strategic reasons. They aren't intended primarily to enrich chief executive officers, other senior executives, bankers and investment bankers but to propel either the buying company and/or the selling company into achieving real growth by the combination of the two businesses. The transaction does, of course, have the ancillary result of enriching the principals involved. But if the result is indeed real growth, both in intention and in reality, the exercise could be a boon to both regional and national economies. What's real growth? Not one that merely adds numbers but which strengthens the companies, adds to the gross domestic product, augments employment and makes the organization more viable and better equipped to survive.

Since all that is no more than a credo for successful business, the principle of strategic mergers is one that guarantees that the number of such transactions will at least remain on a high level and quite possibly increase considerably in the years ahead. My conviction about it is one reason why my chapter on strategic mergers is the longest, most detailed in this book.

Accordingly, there is no American industry that isn't involved to a varying degree in mergers of strategy. But perhaps the most involved are the consumer-goods industries, those which sell the toys, greeting cards, food, clothes and home needs, and those which produce them. Of course, rejecting a bid can also be a strategic move, aimed at protecting the target company's independence. I would like to list briefly a few such strategic combinations, as of this writing, to display their diversity and richness. Besides the standard merger, they also represent investments, leveraged buyouts and acquisitions:

- The United States Playing Card Company, the maker of the Bicycle and Bee brands which was owned by the Frontenac Company of Chicago, was acquired by a group led by management for $140 million. The successful offer kept the company from being sold for the third time in a dozen years. The 127-year old company, employing 800, was bought by Frontenac in 1989 for $95 million. When it was put up for sale in January 1994, it drew 21 bidders. The Cincinnati-based card company produces 70 million decks of cards a year.

  The basic strategy in this deal is merely to keep the company independent and allow it to concentrate without the distraction of being in a heterogeneous organization on building its business and competing against the inexpensive competition from other companies.

- A similar but somewhat different situation involved Younkers Inc., a department store chain in Des Moines with 53 stores in seven Midwest and Western states, which rejected a $152 million buyout offer from Carson Pirie Scott & Company, of Dayton, Ohio. Carson Pirie sought to scoop up a Younkers weakened by a year of disappointing business. But Younkers' board opted to go it alone and hope that the company could grow without a partner. The Carson Pirie

Company was formerly known as the Elder Beerman Stores Corporation, which, incidentally, had itself acquired the famous, old Carson Pirie department stores in the Chicago area and changed its corporate name to the better-known one.

By rejecting Carson Pirie-Elder Beerman, Younkers obviously didn't want to go the route of Carson Pirie in being acquired by Elder Beerman or, for that matter, to join in the trend of fewer but bigger companies so pervasive in American retailing. But how many regional, independent clusters of traditional department stores are left? Younkers decided that it could be one of the few.

- Bristol-Myers Squibb Company, a major pharmaceuticals and health products company, offered $261.5 million for Calgon Vestal Laboratories, a maker of skin-care and infection control products owned by Merck & Company. Bristol-Myers said that the St. Louis-based Calgon will be combined with its Convatec subsidiary in Skillman, New Jersey. This is obviously another market-share extension move.

- Aramark, the park-services company formerly known as ARA Services, said it will pay $130 million in cash to acquire a competitor, the TW Recreational Services division of the Flagstar Companies. Thus, Aramark was adding TW's hotels, restaurants and gift shops at national parks. For Aramark, it was an important expansion move while for Flagstar the transaction satisfied its need to sell off its tangential businesses so that it could concentrate on its core restaurant chains.

- In a health-and-fitness expansion involving a price tag of about $373 million in cash, the Boston-based Bain Capital, an equity investment company, led an investor group to buy the home-fitness equipment and sports-medicine subsidiary of Weider Health and Fitness, of Woodland Hills, California. Bain then merged the purchased businesses into Icon Health and Fitness Inc., Logan, Utah, in which Bain holds a 53 percent interest. The move gives Icon a 25 percent market share of the nation's home-fitness business, one full of promise.

- In a much larger deal, Sybase Inc., an Emeryville, California leader in software for managing corporate databases, announced a $940 million stock exchange for the Power soft Corporation, a specialist software maker in Concord, Massachusetts. In effect, Sybase needed Powersoft to fill a hole in its customer services. Sybase had run into some problems staking its claim for software allowing programmers to develop custom, retrieval applications on their corporate databases. Powersoft was a specialist in that field. Hence, it was a strategic acquisition pure and simple.

Predicting the Future M&A Trend

Almost all the merger experts I interviewed for this book were convinced that the merger boom will continue unabated for the remainder of the 1990s and beyond. Their rationale, their cautions and their opinions differed but the majority agreed on the busy future.

"M&As will continue at a pretty brisk pace. It's such a natural part of the evolution of today's company," says David C. Wittig, co-head of mergers and acquisitions at Salomon Brothers, the investment bankers in New York. "Nothing that I can see can change it from being an important financial tool. Perhaps only government enforcement. But the motivations to sell a business are standard these days and they are well accepted—a management gets old, the CEO becomes ill, the second or third generation wants to cash in the business. And the motivations to buy a business are standard, too. What really drives it is that it is cheaper to buy than to build from the ground up," Wittig said.

He added that if the stock market advances sharply and continues to build, it will hamper the merger-acquisition trend, both in numbers of and value of transactions. "But the fundamentals of the business consolidations or divestitures will basically remain intact and the trend will strengthen again as the market sells off. I don't think that the trend will balloon but it will represent a steady form of business strategy."

Mergers grow in industries that are undergoing change, Wittig adds. This has been true for some time. But now major change is stirring in a number of industries and causing its main players to make strategic moves. He thinks that the industries which will see the most consolidations will be banking and financial institutions, where new regulations have exploded the markets from intrastate banking to nationwide banking; health care where many companies are reorganizing in response to the Administration's strong, though abortive national health-care program; utilities which have been broadly regulated and are now going into deregulation; and defense-aerospace which is undergoing considerable government contract downsizing.

Isn't there a formula for mergers and acquisitions that work? "People who have been successful at it have done it in industries that they know something about," Wittig says, "rather than jump into industries where their lack of knowledge leaves them at risk to competitive change." He went on to say that senior executives involved in buyouts take too long to integrate the acquired company. "Those who have succeeded at it have moved rapidly to integrate the new business and to change the culture."

Clarity and specificity in communications are vital in handling an acquired company, in Wittig's view. "It isn't cruel for the new boss to tell the people in the company he has just bought, 'I own the company now and if that is a problem for you, you might as well get out now.' It's cruel on the other hand *not* to do it. Most people want to be told what to do and that change is coming. It's essential to tell the people up front about the changes. It's the only fair thing to do," Wittig said.

There is a substantial momentum for mergers and acquisitions leading into the last half of the decade, according to Samuel L. Hayes, who holds the Jacob Schiff Chair in Investment Banking at the Harvard Graduate School of Business Administration. "But their form will not be quite the same as in the 1980s," says Professor Hayes. "There will be three separate forms or types. One will be in the restructuring of corporations which began in the 1980s but still has a way to go. But I think these will be restrained by a limitation on debt to buttress the large equity funds making up the investment pools managed by the major investment bankers."

He explained that banks, insurance companies and pension funds will behave more cautiously in financially backing corporate restructuring moves because of the huge defaults on leveraged buyouts and junk bonds, still so well remembered. "The restructuring form that mergers and acquisitions will take will not be so highly leveraged as their counterparts of the 1980s," Professor Hayes said, "and a significant number of them will be spinoffs and rationalizations of former conglomerates."

Another form will represent strategic moves to position companies in rapidly changing industries to be more competitive, he said, "and we've already seen a bunch of those." After recently returning from Saudi Arabia, he said that he had talked there to the local manager of a "Big Eight" accounting firm. "I asked him, 'It's hard to imagine why your firm would have 7,000 to 8,000 employees and as many as 1,500 partners. Isn't that very cumbersome?' The manager told me, 'Not at all. It's essential that we remain competitive. It's also essential that accounting firms such as ours do more in-depth consulting for increasingly global clients. That requires substantial staff and substantial supervision. No, it's not cumbersome.'"

Another form of M&As in the rest of the 1990s will be "logical combinations of financial service companies, particularly banks—logical because of the fragmented banking industry which has been regulated not by legislative fiat but by administrative regulation," Professor Hayes said. "Now it is being unregulated and creating what is essentially national banking and is further eroding the Chinese Wall between banking and investment banking. Now the big banks and insurance companies are doing securities business which they were barred from for decades. What it means, of course, are much more consolidations in the entire field of financial services."

Does he have any concerns about the encroaching bigness of business mergers? "No, I don't because of the constant redefining of the marketplace," he said. "Global markets are changing the parameters of the past. Nowadays, medium-sized companies shop all over the world for credit. There's no such thing anymore as strictly regional or national markets."

One of the most prominent lawyers on the M&A scene, Allen Finkelson, senior partner of Cravath, Swaine & Moore, the New York law firm, believes like David Wittig that the future trend in business consolidations greatly depends upon the volatility of the stock market.

"Most deals nowadays are corporate, synergistic deals involving a lot of stock, although it's quite true that the banks certainly are back in the money-lending business," he said. "If the stock market goes down, given the banks' penchant for putting up a lot of money, the banks may hesitate to finance deals to the same extent as before. The point is that more cash will be needed in those high-price deals which involve a lot of stock."

He said that principals in M&As tend not to use their own stock while using cash in deals becomes an expensive proposition. "And we must conclude that if stock values decline and cash is tougher to get, the prices of deals should go up," Finkelson said.

So, if the market falls, more cash will be needed and the incidence of hostile deals will also rise, he added. "The raid is difficult to do with stock because there's just too much uncertainty about the stock values," he said, "but when that uncertainty vanishes the hostile deal seems more viable."

Hence, says Finkelson, the stock market will be the key factor in future transactions. But will government enforcement wield a more important role than it has in the last 14 years? He said that the Clinton administration has been more active on enforcement than the prior two administrations but it was not likely to become more so in its remaining two years. Will the new Republican control of both houses be more supportive of business consolidations? "I don't think that the change in the political picture will have anything to do with enforcement," Finkelson said. "There will be just too many other issues to settle without that."

Brian Finn, managing director of the First Boston Corporation, New York, and co-head of its mergers and acquisition practice, notes that the recent general trends in mergers have been along industry lines. He particularly cited healthcare, financial services, defense and aerospace and media. "I certainly think that the same general trend will prevail over the near- to mid-term," he says.

But he also feels that the movement in interest rates will impact the rate of transactions, adversely if they rise much and positively if they remain stable, but especially if they decline.

He is convinced that foreign mergers will grow. "Over the next couple of years, the improving European economies will mean that European companies will be acquiring companies on the continent and elsewhere," Finn says, "and also will be the recipient of bids and investments from other countries."

But in the U.S. where a tide is developing within the much revitalized Republican party to reduce the capital gains tax, Finn says, "It will be less important in terms of the merger trend than economic issues. A capital gains tax reduction may stimulate some M&As but not significantly."

Asked for his opinion about some of the bigger deals of recent years, Finn said that "the RJR Nabisco deal looks bad at this point. But it's easy to criticize a deal after the fact. Sony Corporation doesn't look good in its writeoff on its Hollywood movie acquisitions but people tend to forget how well its purchases into American music have done."

Government activity? "Well, you would think that if you have a Democratic President and a Republican Congress, there would be a standoff," Finn said. "But the President can still name the chairman of the Federal Trade Commission and the Assistant Attorney General for Antitrust Enforcement. They would be the ones to decide how tough to get in the area of mergers and acquisitions. I think that the Federal Trade Commission has been very hard on Eli Lilly, BAT Industries and Tele-Communications, compared to what the previous administrations did. But I don't think that that will last."

One of the most enthusiastic among those interviewed about the future of M&As was Bernard Jacobs, the senior vice president of Chase Manhattan Corporation and head of its global acquisition activities.

"The future will make the peak 1980s look like just the beginning," he said. "This will bring it to the next level—globalization. The wide perception of the global economy will cause companies to think in terms of much larger size. A business cannot be a $150 million company in a global market and survive. A cable company with 150,000 subscribers acquiring just another cable company like itself wouldn't be able to compete."

Jacobs sees globalization leading to many other types of change.

"The United States will see European companies talking much more to the issue of focusing on core businesses," he said. "Companies in Germany, Japan and other highly developed countries will no longer feel that just because they owned certain businesses, even their own company for 50 years, they should own it for another 50. Foreign companies which are highly diversified will find it necessary to concentrate on fewer businesses. Whereas if they had 10 divisions, they will wind up with three or four. They may have had the other seven for a century because 'divestiture' was not in their vocabulary. Now, as they try to compete in the global economy, it will make sense to them to concentrate on fewer businesses and make their mark in them."

Steven Wolitzer, co-head of mergers and acquisitions at Lehman Brothers, the New York-based investment banking house, observes, "We've seen a huge pickup in mergers and acquisitions in the last year or two. I see it as a strong trend for the next two to three years. Beyond that, you have to predict economic cycles if you want to predict M&As."

In the past, Wolitzer says, the U.S. economy's pattern was followed closely by the trend of M&As. "In the 1980s, the economic cycle turned into a worldwide recession and the U.S. suffered through a huge slowdown. The year of 1989 was the last bull year," he said, "but 1990, 1991 and 1992 were affected by the slowdown of the 1980s. We saw the start of a resurgence in 1993. The 1994 year has seen an extremely active M&A trend due to a strong national economy. The M&A rate also grew in Europe and Asia in the last year except for Japan which is still weathering an economic slowdown."

But a number of other factors are pushing the number of business consolidations, Wolitzer said, such as executives and companies responding to the increasing impact of global markets, trying to establish international factories and new market share. In addition, restructuring moves in the U.S., while beginning to slow up, have led to more mergers and acquisitions. Europe, too, is starting to catch up in the restructuring of companies. A third factor, said Wolitzer, is the "tremendous dynamism in certain industries, such as media and telecommunications. In those two industries, everyone seems to be staking out their claims in broadcast, media, cellular phones and satellite broadcasting.

"At the same time, the most dynamic industries are healthcare, which is thoroughly reforming itself, and financial services where new vistas are opening because of more liberal government regulation," he said. "The food and beverage industries are both enjoying more global demand so that we can expect many more cross-border deals," Wolitzer continued. "And the same for the energy businesses where there are certainly more consolidations."

Beyond all that, he said, "the one common theme in consolidations among all American industries is strategic motivation. No one any more is buying a company because it's cheap and they are willing to pay for a good bargain. Companies on the selling block will certainly get cheaper if the stock market retrenches. But that won't much change the basic strategic drive."

A somewhat more moderate approach was taken by Laurence S. Grafstein, head of the telecommunications and media practice at Wasserstein, Perella & Company, investment bankers in New York.

He said, "The M&As trend, broadly defined, is probably sustainable. I include in the broad trend not just strategic mergers but spinoffs and privatizations." But Grafstein agreed with the others on the stimulus provided by technological improvements, regulatory change and the global economy. Foreseeing a much intensified international competition, he said that American business will have to sharpen its focus to capture a place in that arena. "Half the world will be coming into a market economy," Grafstein said, "which will raise the competitive levels and force companies to allocate their capital in a way to enhance their competitive posture."

But this will curb capital sources making money more expensive to borrow, he believes. "Because of this, companies will have to be more selective on how they spend their borrowings and that should help to stimulate mergers and acquisitions," Grafstein said.

Another more restrained forecaster was Ralph Nelson, professor of economics at Queens College of the City University of New York, who said, "I speculate that the erratic stock market and the bad experience of many mergers may level out the merger trend of this era. I suspect that we are not coming into a big merger wave but one of more smaller, strategic mergers. They will be motivated by ordinary business expansion drives and efforts to maintain or increase profits," he added.

Rebutting Those Forecasts and Those Opinions

Nothing is easier than masticating someone else's comments. Still in a state of speculation, the forecasts of the eight quoted earlier nonetheless do mostly make both sense and logic. They are partly based on facts that we know today but depend much more on future events as well as future prevailing business thinking. Thus, commenting on speculative observations can only be speculative, in itself. So here goes:

David Wittig of Salomon Brothers: If "mergers are such a natural part of the evolution of today's company," doesn't this risk the absence of a basic strategy that should impart its own life and strength to a business? In other words, anyone can buy or sell but not everyone can come up with a stream of consistent innovation. So what is U.S. business, a creative force or a broker of others' companies?

Also, "People who have been successful at it (acquisitions) have done it in industries that they know something about." True enough. But then why are so many horizontal acquisitions eventually ineffective and overturned? I suspect it is because ego ultimately gets into the way of better judgment, faulty chemistry does its damage and it isn't very long before both sides wonder why they got hitched in the first place.

I like David's remarks, especially the "it's the only fair thing to do."

Professor Samuel Hayes of the Harvard Graduate School: I like the Saudi Arabia story but that ratio of one partner in the accounting firm to every five or six employees worries me. Doesn't it make for excessive supervision, too much looking over the workers' shoulders or, perhaps, too much executive-rank-and-file fraternizing?

Hayes' discussion of the three forms of M&As for the balance of the decade interested me because it seemed logical. The term "rationalizations" seems very pertinent in this latest wave of M&As. But I am not so sure I want to buy stocks and bonds from a bank as yet. Not until they pay better interest on savings or certificates of deposit.

Allen Finkelson: "Never argue with a lawyer" is probably a good motto to follow. But Finkelson, as I learned from past experience, is special, honest and tough. I agree with him that if the stock market falls, more cash will be needed and there will be more hostile deals. But I can't agree with Allen that the Republican Congress won't have any effect on government enforcement. I think it will have an effect—even less enforcement.

Brian Finn of First Boston: Recent merger trends definitely have been along industry lines, as Brian says, but I am not sure that future mergers will be based on either the four industries he cites or on the horizontal concept. I think that the whole area of travel and recreation will boom as will the service industries in either cross-border transactions or in a vertical aspect—or both. Brian may be right that a reduced capital gains tax may not significantly stimulate M&As but it will make a lot of businesspeople ecstatic.

Bernard Jacobs of Chase Manhattan: What Bernie says about globalization becoming the next level in mergers and acquisitions rings true. And focusing on core businesses is way overdue, anyway. But if German and Japanese companies no longer feel that deep conviction about owning their companies or all their divisions for years and years, what does this hold for their loyal employees? Will they be heading into the same people dislocation problems that the U.S. has?

Steven Wolitzer of Lehman Brothers: Why hedge on economic cycles? Who knows more about them than Lehman Brothers? Certainly M&As will reflect the economy's turns and shifts but what will they be? But that aside, I like what he says about everyone in media and telecommunications staking their claim in all of it. Is that good? Don't specialists do a better job than generalists? I wonder if, ultimately, the U.S. won't be getting back into another conglomerate binge? It never quite went fully underground, did it?

Laurence Grafstein of Wasserstein, Perella: I can't agree with his forecast of a limited growth of M&As. It will be much stronger, in my humble view. But I very much like his point about half the world "coming into a market economy" and what sharp effect it will have on competitive levels and capital allocation. And, of course, the need to sharpen a company's focus.

Professor Ralph Nelson of Queens College: Aside from the excellent points on merger philosophy mentioned in chapter 5, I cannot agree with him that the strategic mergers to come will be small transactions. With economic rates spurting around the world, with our interest rates going up and inflation raising its flaming head, M&As have got to be bigger and bigger.

So How Big Can M&As Get?

Who owns America?

We all do. And the government does. But suppose, just suppose that someone with all that wherewithal or the ability to generate that wherewithal wanted to buy, say, Rhode Island? Or Maine? Or California? And had the marketing savvy to build in some really great incentives? And suppose that someone or some people decided not just to stop at a few states but to go for the whole ballgame?

Here's what lawyers tell me: The country is indeed owned by the people and the various governments. We wrested it from the British and the Mexicans in wars and bought the rest in pieces from the Indians and the French. The government, in turn, has sold land to private individuals who have built, farmed, grazed or let it go fallow. But the government has also retained considerable land and built many structures on it. Highways, tunnels and bridges are owned either by the local community, the state or the federal government.

So that's who owns America, the people and the government. And that's why any potential buyer would, like most commercial merger players, have to set up a two-tier purchase, a tender offer to the populace and a tender offer to the government. One of these might even force the hand of the other by taking the initiative.

Are mergers and acquisitions getting so big in size and value that such a premise is not just a fantasy? Its an interesting thought.

Is there enough money in the world to carry it out? No, but it can be generated by some creative investment vehicles. Would people ever sell their birthright for a few paltry dollars? Maybe, if the dollar amount was much greater than "paltry." Would the federal government then find itself pushed into a corner by the will of its own citizens? It wouldn't be the first time. Would the government then be so pressured that it would give in to a not-so-tender offer? Who can say for sure?

index

229